P9-CJC-914

RIVERSIDE PUBLIC LIBRARY
FOUNDATION
Donated in honor of
Jamie Robinson
for service on the
Board of Directors
Jan. 2003-Dec. 2009

Staying True

Staying True

JENNY SANFORD

BALLANTINE BOOKS / NEW YORK

Published in the United States by Ballantine Books, an imprint of The Random House Publishing Group, a division of Random House, Inc., New York.

BALLANTINE and colophon are registered trademarks of Random House, Inc.

ISBN 978-0-345-52239-9

Wedding photos reprinted with permission of Davidoff Studios, Inc.

Photo of First Lady playing soccer reprinted with permission of Anne McQuary/www.heybabysmile.com

Photo of First Lady and Governor Sanford at inauguration reprinted with permission of State Media Company/Tim Dominick

Photo of First Family at prayer service reprinted with permission of State Media Company

Printed in the United States of America on acid-free paper

www.ballantinebooks.com

2 4 6 8 9 7 5 3 1

First Edition

Book design by Susan Turner

For Marshall, Landon, Bolton, and Blake with all my love to you, my greatest gifts from above

PROLOGUE

I SEE NOW THAT JUNE 24, 2009, WAS A DAY THAT CHANGED FOREVER the trajectory of my life, but it did not change me.

I woke up early that day, as I have always done during our summers at the beach. The boys and I were at our house on Sullivan's Island, where we had moved when the school year ended a few weeks earlier. My mornings there began with a sunrise cup of coffee in the hour before the boys woke. I savored that quiet time alone as the kitchen filled with light and I wrote in my journal. I jotted thoughts, rarely a narrative of events, and usually reflected on a passage of scripture. My devotions had become more urgent and searching in the six months since I discovered that my husband, Mark Sanford, the governor of South Carolina, was having an affair with a woman in Argentina.

As I sat on a stool at the kitchen island writing, I knew Mark's flight from Buenos Aires was about to touch down. He had been out of the state (though the world didn't yet know how far he'd wandered) for several days. The media and his political opponents were asking pointed questions about where he was, but only a few reporters had called me. Being on Sullivan's—two hours away from the state capital, Columbia—was a blessing on that front. I'd found out only the day before that Mark was in South America. Within hours, the world would know, and the press would be hovering at the end of our driveway.

The truth was that Mark and I had been quietly separated and had not spoken for two weeks, at my request, with clear restrictions on contact with the Argentinean woman he had started an affair with a year earlier. If he and I were to have a chance at reconciliation, he agreed not to contact her or the boys and me while he sorted things out. Cut off this way, I hoped, Mark might understand what it would be like to lose his family in the form he'd always known it. I wanted Mark to ache for what he'd always said mattered most to him. I thought he got it. Before he left to "get his head right," as he'd explained it to the boys, he looked me straight in the eye and said, "I will not see her." That morning I knew he had broken that promise.

My prayers were brief but pointed: "Lord give me strength. Lord let Mark find you. Lord protect our boys." So many times, I had prayed for the patience to wait this out, or for understanding for him and for me. I felt the full weight of the day ahead on my shoulders. This time when I clasped my hands and shut my eyes, I prayed that the Lord would grant me the strength to protect our children in the ugly time ahead, and I prayed for Mark who was clearly lost.

The only one of the four boys at home that morning was thirteen-year-old Bolton, who was about to leave for a day of fishing with his uncle and cousin. As he gobbled down his breakfast, I pictured our dear friend and Mark's long-time aide, Chris Allen, picking up Mark at the Atlanta airport. A loyal young man who had recently tied his business goals to Mark's political future, Chris had driven through the night to be there when Mark landed. By now, they were on the road to Columbia. I wondered if Mark understood that the whole country, it seemed, wanted a full description of his "hiking the Appalachian Trail."

The phone rang. It was Mark calling from the car. "Hey, how are you?" he asked quietly.

"How am I? How do you think I am?" I sighed.

"Jenny, be gentle with me," he said in a tired voice.

"Gentle?" I asked incredulously. "Do you know what kind of a storm you are returning to? And where do we stand?"

"The good news is it's over now," he said of his affair, and then added, "I've already met a reporter at the airport and told her of my love of adventure travel and so on. I'll call you after I get to Columbia."

I asked again, "What about us?"

"I told you it's all behind us . . . everything's good."

Good?! What part of this did he think was good? I wondered.

I had been anticipating this call, searching for the right way to respond, but everything about his manner caught me off guard, beginning with his blasé tone. I don't know what he could have said to soothe me, but at least I expected an apology and some expression of regret. I hadn't detected a note of that in his voice. He was riding down the highway with Chris arranging for a press conference later that morning and I was one of a number of things he was dealing with. By the time we hung up, I hoped it was slowly dawning on him that this story about his "adventure" wasn't going to hold.

There had been many a morning in the six months since I discovered his affair when I had cried about the state of my marriage, and just as many evenings spent praying with my two girlfriends Frannie and Lalla Lee. This morning, at least, I wasn't going to cry. I was the one who needed to get my head right. I grabbed my iPod, smeared on some sunblock, and headed out the back gate to the beach, some two hundred yards away.

The sun was moving quickly higher in the slate blue sky and the air was hot and sticky, but that thickness didn't dim the sparkle of the sea. My spirit lifted as soon as I set my flip-flops in the sand. Orange and yellow wildflowers lined the path behind our house that leads to the shore. "His Strength Is Perfect" was the first tune on my iPod, which helped my spirits too, as I emerged from the corridor of low dunes and saw the broad beach before me.

This was not in my control, not in my hands, I thought, as the song changed to "I Can Only Imagine." What my future held was something I, the woman who always thought years ahead, now couldn't imagine. Could I imagine a life without Mark, the man whose ambitions had been the center of all that we had done as a family for twenty years? Without him, what was our direction? And how did he feel about me now that he had seen her? Once we got through this day, both of us had life-changing decisions to make. I walked more quickly along the shore, smiling when I saw dolphins playing in the surf. At the beach, I feel wondrously small; my problems are insignificant in this big, beautiful world. This would all sort itself out, and at some point, I would know what to do next. I felt certain of that and that only. I breathed steadily, more deeply, and drank in the peace the sea affords, a tremendous luxury in a world and life otherwise very public.

When I returned, I found that Lalla Lee Campsen, one of my oldest friends in South Carolina, had let herself in. Of course she was there. I could have guessed that she would be from the moment I turned up the path home. She sat at the kitchen island with a notepad and a pen, fielding calls. Petite, bright-eyed, and always smiling, Lalla Lee was the first of Mark's childhood friends to embrace me when this Midwestern Catholic girl found herself living in the Deep South. In those carefree days before politics consumed my time, we'd boated together and played many sets of tennis. Our boys had become good friends, almost as close as Lalla Lee and I had. I was grateful for her steady presence. Whatever this day brought me, we would face it together.

I heard the door to the carport slam and went to the top of the stairs to see Frannie Reese, my closest friend on the island, sprinting upstairs toward me, a bundle of energy in her shorts and bathing suit. She had two cups from Starbucks and handed me one. When we first moved to Sullivan's Island back in 1998, Frannie's husband, Tim, was away almost as much as Mark had been during his years serving in Congress. She and I started out as carpool pals, but within months we were picking up each other's kids after school, taking them to appointments and to practices and eating dinner frequently at each other's homes, herding our kids around like one big mob. Recently, when my sister Kathy moved to Charleston and had a baby of her own, she fell seamlessly into Frannie's generosity. Frannie came to see how I was doing that morning. She said she'd be back before Mark's press conference. I retreated to shower and freshen up.

As I finished getting dressed, I heard Kathy's boisterous voice filling the main room as she came through the front door. She's an artist with a wicked sense of humor who, like our mom, knows how to make an entrance. "He wasn't hiking the Appalachian Trail," she announced. "He was getting Argentine tail!" I laughed. How good it felt to laugh!

Unbidden, my local sisterhood had assembled itself at my house, and my sister Gier was on the plane here from Chicago. So, too, was my dad, who would be arriving within an hour or two. I thought of Blake and Landon, ages ten and fifteen, four miles off the coast deep-sea fishing with Lalla Lee's sons and a friend, and Marshall, our oldest, in the Caribbean, for a two-week summer job. I paused next to the bed that Mark and I shared, to appreciate how truly I loved and was loved and how nothing that happened that day could take any of that from me.

Out in the kitchen, Kathy and Lalla Lee urged me to eat, but I had no appetite. We picked at the salads that Kathy thought to bring. The phone continued to ring, but we were screening the calls. It seemed we were hunkered down in a safe zone, in our cinder-block fortress by the sea, waiting for the next shoe to drop.

"So, Jenny, while you were in the shower Mark called again," Lalla Lee told me reluctantly.

"Are you kidding?" Kathy said, grinning at me. "I gave him a piece of my mind when I answered Jenny's cell. Of course, he thought I was her for a while."

I shook my head, imagining what Kathy had let loose on Mark. Kathy and I have had our sisterly spats, but we are fiercely protective of each other. I felt safer with her around.

After lunch, Chris Allen patched through Mark, who was polling those he trusted on how much he should reveal.

"Should I tell everything?" he asked, businesslike still.

"Whatever you think is right," I said. "What does Lerner say?" I asked, referring to our longtime media adviser and friend in DC.

"He says not to get into too much detail," Mark sighed.

"I agree with that. But you have to be honest about where you were and why."

This was Mark at the mansion and in work mode. I had long ago come to understand that private talk would have to wait.

The day before, when I knew for certain that Mark was in Argentina, I reached out to my family in Chicago, and my dad volunteered to fly to Charleston to be at my side, as had Gier. In the coming weeks, there would be a time when I would need my mom's lively spirit and take-charge attitude, but that day I needed Dad and his calm. I was folding laundry mindlessly, trying to keep busy, when he pulled into the driveway. Just the sight of him, tidy in his pressed khakis and golf shirt, made me feel more firmly anchored to the ground. Yet all I could manage was a weak smile when he walked through the door. Since Mark confessed his affair to him a few weeks earlier, Dad and I had spoken many times. Now we hugged, not saying much. Up close, I saw the pain he carried in his eyes. I was not sure what there was to say.

Mark called again, first announcing that the press conference would be later in the afternoon.

"*The State* has some of our emails," he admitted. I understood that the "our" of that statement did not refer to me, but to his correspondence with his lover. If they were anything like the racy letter I'd discovered in Mark's desk that January, I needed to brace myself for another public humiliation.

"How many do they have? How long have they had them?"

"I don't know."

So, my best political, if not spousal, advice: "Well, be honest and get it over with. Whatever you do, don't talk about your heart."

Then Gier arrived with her boys and mimicked how she had waved as they drove past the reporters and photographers who slumped, bored, in the driveway. It was time for Mark's press conference, and we all crammed into my bedroom, some holding hands as we watched Mark enter the Capitol rotunda. He walked, distracted and guilty, to the podium, squirming, not knowing how to begin. Frannie is the type who likes to ask questions and she started up. I had to caution her that I wanted to hear every word. We were somber and a little frightened as Mark started to ramble. He spent considerable time—it seemed like an eternity—apologizing to everyone in his life, every citizen of the state, people of faith all over the world. Then he revealed the state of his heart. He described days spent crying in Argentina with his lover.

I still don't quite know why I wanted to hear every syllable, but it felt important to bear witness to this in real time, to hear what the watching public was hearing. That said, I am grateful to this day that I can't remember much of it. While it was going on, I was in such shock, it felt as though this was happening to someone else. I wished that were true. Out the bedroom window, I saw a bright orange container ship heading out to sea on its way to Turkey or China. What I wouldn't have given to be on it!

Finally, no longer able to stand the sight of Mark pining

away with tears streaming down his face, Kathy looked at Lalla Lee and said exactly what all of us were thinking, "Will you call someone and tell them to please pull him away from that camera?" Lalla Lee called Chris Allen to suggest this, but the press conference did not end.

As Mark carried on, Kathy moaned, "Let's just end this!"

As if taking a cue from his vocal sister-in-law, Mark did finally finish, but then the commentators began talking about "another politician who cheated on his wife." Wronged Political Spouses is a list no one wants to be on, but now my name would be featured there. Immediately my cell phone rang. It was Mark. Lalla returned to the kitchen to handle the house phone and Frannie went too, to make dinner. I took the call on the porch.

"How'd I do?" he asked.

"Are you kidding me? You cried for her and said little of me or of the boys." I guess he'd forgotten I was not the one to praise this performance.

We hung up, and I went to the study above my bedroom for some privacy. I wanted to say something, to respond, to react, even though I knew that was not the usual protocol followed by betrayed political wives. I'd already missed the part in this ritual where I would stand with head bowed next to him in front of hundreds of cameras as he made his shameful admission. (If I'd been there, perhaps he'd have gotten off the stage sooner.) I had never considered myself a traditional political spouse, though, and this wasn't the moment to start being one. I had been working on a statement.

The night before, over dinner at the Campsens, we had discussed what I could say. Once home, I wrote a formal one-page statement. Now I reviewed what I'd written to see if it still reflected what I felt. It did. I wasn't ashamed and I wanted no one's pity. I asked my dad to read my statement and he suggested a few minor adjustments. Those done, I sent it to my assistant in the First Lady's Office, who emailed it to the local and national press. I also walked down the driveway and handed it to the reporters gathered there. Handing over my statement gave me a wonderful sense of release. I knew there would be endless requests for interviews in the coming days and weeks, and Mark and I would engage in more painful conversations. For that moment, though, my thinking was complete. I truly believed I would be able to enjoy a relaxed dinner with my family, and I really couldn't wait to hug the boys as they returned home. I knew in my heart that whether I reconciled with my husband or not, saying what I truly felt at this time of personal crisis would begin a new chapter in my life. I did what seemed reasonable to me and it seems to have opened new doors: doors to sharing, doors to friendship, doors to some kind of peace.

STATEMENT FROM FIRST LADY JENNY SANFORD
(RELEASED 5:19 P.M., JUNE 24, 2009)

I would like to start by saying I love my husband and I believe I have put forth every effort possible to be the best wife I can be during our almost twenty years of marriage. As well, for the last fifteen years my husband has been fully engaged in public service to the citizens and taxpayers of this state and I have faithfully supported him in those efforts to the best of my ability. I have been and remain proud of his accomplishments and his service to this state.

I personally believe that the greatest legacy I will leave behind in this world is not the job I held on Wall Street, or the campaigns I managed for Mark, or the work I have done as First Lady or even the philanthropic activities in which I have been routinely engaged. Instead, the greatest legacy I will leave in this world is the character of the children I, or we, leave behind. It is for that reason that I deeply regret the recent actions of my husband Mark and their potential damage to our children.

I believe wholeheartedly in the sanctity, dignity, and importance of the institution of marriage. I believe that has been consistently reflected in my actions. When I found out about my husband's infidelity I worked immediately to first seek reconciliation through forgiveness, and then to work diligently to repair our marriage. We reached a point where I felt it was important to look my sons in the eyes and maintain my dignity, self-respect, and my basic sense of right and wrong. I therefore asked my husband to leave two weeks ago.

This trial separation was agreed to with the goal

of ultimately strengthening our marriage. During this short separation it was agreed that Mark would not contact us. I kept this separation quiet out of respect of his public office and reputation, and in hopes of keeping our children from just this type of public exposure. Because of this separation, I did not know where he was in the past week.

I believe enduring love is primarily a commitment and an act of will and for a marriage to be successful, that commitment must be reciprocal. I believe Mark has earned a chance to resurrect our marriage.

Psalm 127 states that sons are a gift from the Lord and children a reward from Him. I will continue to pour my energy into raising our sons to be honorable young men. I remain willing to forgive Mark completely for his indiscretions and to welcome him back, in time, if he continues to work toward reconciliation with a true spirit of humility and repentance.

This is a very painful time for us and I would humbly request now that members of the media respect the privacy of my boys and me as we struggle together to continue on with our lives and as I seek the wisdom of Solomon, the strength and patience of Job, and the grace of God in helping to heal my family.

Staying True

ONE

As I maneuvered the unfamiliar Honda hatchback through the foggy roads of South Carolina's lowcountry, I wondered why I was making this torturous journey to see Mark Sanford. It was 1987, and I'd only been on a handful of dates with him, dates that were not overwhelmingly romantic. One such date was brunch with my parents (not exactly a recipe for romance) in New York around Thanksgiving. Shortly thereafter, he'd invited me to spend New Year's Eve weekend with him and his family at their farm on the South Carolina coast. I had found the invitation intriguing because it was unexpected and because Mark was different from the men I'd dated before. I asked my mom for her two cents.

"He seems like a nice young man and you should go see

him," she said. "Go to South Carolina, it will be fun no matter what. And I'll bet he has nice friends!"

I certainly agreed with her that it would be an adventure either way. Little did I know . . .

Mark had told me where to look for the car in the Charleston airport parking lot and that the directions for the fifty-mile drive to Coosaw, the family farm, would be on a clipboard on the passenger seat. I hadn't anticipated the car would be a stick shift. Though I'd tried before, I didn't really know how to drive a stick.

When I was a teenager, my friend Julie and I had tried to teach ourselves to drive a manual transmission truck on untraveled back roads and small-town streets in northern Wisconsin. We laughed as we stalled and stalled, hardly able to go a few feet without having to start the truck again. We got around a bit, but we'd never taken the truck out in traffic and only drove in daylight. All these years later, I remembered the general idea and, with some bucking and stalling and squealing of wheels—and some out-loud questioning what I'd gotten myself into—I made it out of the airport as directed.

I had first met Mark seven months earlier, on Memorial Day weekend in the Hamptons, a summer destination for many young New Yorkers. My friend Moira and I had taken the train from Manhattan out to a house we were renting with a few other women, and we needed a ride to meet up with some friends at a party. Mark had driven to Long Island from Manhattan, where he had a summer job at Goldman Sachs. He and his friend Bob were dispatched to pick us up, arriving in this same beat-up two-door hatchback. The car seemed way too small for Mark's tall, lanky frame, and with all of us packed in, it was a very tight fit indeed.

There was something attractive to me about Mark right from the start. I was used to Wall Street's suspender-snapping braggarts, the kind of men I met often in the mergers and acquisitions department at the investment banking firm, Lazard Frères and Co., where I worked. Mark was pleasant and soft-spoken. We exchanged phone numbers and I remember hoping this southern gentleman would someday call. But I have to admit that I met other men that summer who inspired that hope in me. We were all young—I was 24—that summer and I didn't think that this would turn into something long-term.

I tried to picture that charming southern man as I continued on my frustrating journey to see him. The Honda stalled out twice before I got onto Highway 17 and headed south. The road was narrow with innumerable potholes and obscured by thick lowcountry fog. I charted my progress by the few signs I saw along the way, noting towns with names such as Red Top, Ravenel, and Edisto. My knuckles turned white as I gripped the stick, keeping the car in third gear the whole way. I was afraid to shift gears, slow down, or stop, terrified of hitting a deer or alligator or one of the other creatures Mark had told me might be around these parts. This was a long way from Manhattan, and a longer way still from where I grew up in Chicago.

As I drove, I had plenty of time to consider Mark's intentions in inviting me to meet his family and ring in the New

Year. It wasn't entirely clear if he was interested in me romantically; making me drive myself didn't suggest that I was someone he was dying to see. Our time together in New York had been fun and engaging and, by this point, there was a flirtatious attraction between us, but things hadn't progressed to true romance. I still wasn't thinking long-term about him. What was he doing? What was I doing? After about forty-five minutes, I carefully pulled over when I saw a phone booth in Jacksonboro, then scarcely a town, with only a gas station and a closed-down restaurant. I tried to call Mark, but no one answered at Coosaw. I was thankful I also had the phone number of the home in Yemassee, where the New Year's Eve pig roast was being held. I got the hostess, Evie Chace, on the phone and explained my situation.

"Good God, you're by yourself in Jacksonboro!" she exclaimed. Evie told me that Mark was already at the party—he'd left Coosaw without waiting for me. She gave me directions to her house and said she would let Mark know I was on my way.

I arrived to the party well underway. Evie—wearing a necklace of blinking Christmas lights (how could I not love her immediately?)—welcomed me warmly and began to introduce me around conspiratorily: "This is Jenny, Mark's date. Can you believe he left his car for her at the airport and she made it here on her own on a night like this?!"

Gradually I found my way around the room to Mark and his family. Mark gave me a peck on the cheek and coolly said, "Hey. Glad you made it" as though I'd just stopped in from down the street. He was completely relaxed and enjoying the party, not particularly focused on me or my comfort. Truth to tell, I started looking around for those cute friends Mom thought he might have.

Another handsome young man greeted me. He offered his hand politely, "Bill Sanford. Nice to meet you. You must be Jenny."

"I am," I responded, "and I am so glad to be here and not in that Honda."

"Can I get you some wine?" asked Mark.

It's about time! I thought. "Yes, thanks, that would be nice."

Mark disappeared momentarily to get me a glass, and I began to look around the crowded dining room. As I scanned the room, I saw a woman who looked a lot like me, but dressed in tweedy hunting attire. She introduced herself.

"You muuust be Jenny!" she said, with dramatic emphasis. She continued: "I cannot believe Mark left a car for you. I'm *Saah*rah Sanford and we are all so excited to meet you."

"That wasn't a problem," I said. "I just wish I knew how to drive stick!"

"John Sanford. Nice to meet you. You mean you really don't know how to drive stick? What did you do?" asked another Sanford clone.

"I just drove," I said, matter-of-factly.

"Our brother can be such a piiig!" said Sarah.

Mark and his siblings looked so much alike with their dark brown hair, warm hazel eyes, and just the right amount of freckles. What a good-looking family, I thought. As the wine hit my system and the warmth of the room and the people swept over me, I began to unwind from the harrowing drive, leaving my New York intensity behind. Mark started to introduce me around with pride, showing genuine interest in me. I was glad I had not complained about the drive or drawn attention to the strain I left behind when I entered the party. I felt I had just passed some test with Mark, and not complaining about what I'd endured was part of it.

After cocktails, Mark found me a jacket to wear when we went outside to sit around picnic tables draped in red-and-white checkered cloths. Dinner was roast pig and slaw, a delicious traditional South Carolinian feast that I would come to eat my fair share of in the years ahead. Mark said he had been celebrating New Year's Eve at Evie's with these folks as long as he could remember. This was just the type of familial gathering that was missing in my New York banking life, so far from my own family and home. Mark and I held hands by the open fire as fireworks exploded over the rice fields just beyond.

After leaving the party, we drove a short distance to Coosaw; blessedly, Mark took the wheel. He had described the farm as rough and tumble, yet beautiful. By the time we arrived, however, I could barely see anything in the pitch-black night. We formally welcomed the New Year with a sweet midnight kiss alone on a dock overlooking the river, the fog hovering close over the water.

As I fell asleep that night in a small cabin not far from the main house, the pride I felt from having passed the test fell

tures as if they were old friends and wasn't at all anxious about the alligators he spotted nestled in the pluff mud for warmth. City girl that I was—and largely still am—I thought they were logs at the water's edge.

As the sun rose, I soaked in the magical beauty of Coosaw, a large tract along a tidal basin just past the mouth of the Combahee River. The sparkling waters of the river served as a backdrop for palmettos and large live oak trees draped with clumps of gently swinging Spanish moss that surrounded us. This was a place outside of time, a world that filled me with peace. But I was seduced by more than the natural beauty of the landscape. I could see that this was where Mark's heart resided, and as it became clear what the place had meant to him over the years, I began to see it in the same way.

Mark was a junior in high school when his father was diagnosed with ALS and the family—Mark, his two brothers, sister, and their mother—moved from Florida to their summer home on Coosaw, the place they thought he'd be happiest in his final days. Although the doctors had given his father only six months to live, his dad died almost six years later when Mark was finishing his undergraduate degree. The eldest of his siblings, Mark went to great effort to save this family home. As his father declined, his focus on spending all his time with the family kept him from preparing financially for what would happen after he died. When his father passed, Mark discovered how expensive it was to maintain the farm and understood that he needed to raise money immediately to pay ongoing farm expenses and the inheritance taxes.

away a bit and I began to wonder why I had to be tested at all. Tonight it seemed Mark was actively testing my mettle, assessing my tolerance for what exactly I didn't know. There still seemed to be a lot I didn't know about him. But even as I was uncertain about him, I certainly was interested and wanted to know more.

I knew that Mark's father, a surgeon, had died after a long battle with Lou Gehrig's disease (ALS) when Mark was still in college. He was buried at Coosaw, sacred ground for the Sanford family. Mark was now in his last year of the graduate business program at the University of Virginia, and I could tell he was driven; he talked about a big future for himself in real estate. But I didn't have a sense of his dreams beyond his ambitions; yet knowing about those dreams suddenly seemed of interest to me.

I have always thought of love as more than just a feeling. To me love is a verb, an action that you engage in every day through the things you do for those you cherish. I had had a serious relationship in college and thought I was really in love. In time, that feeling faded, and my commitment wore thin. In my first years on Wall Street, I'd had a few brief relationships, some more intense than others. As a result, I knew what it felt like to look one day at a man I had strong feelings for and realize I couldn't possibly spend my life with him. I didn't want that kind of relationship anymore.

Mark's even-keeled nature was part of the intrigue for me. Perhaps developing a friendship with Mark before the sparks began to fly was part of his appeal. Gradually getting to know each other, slowly opening our hearts was novel to me personally and suggested the kind of old-fashioned love I'd heard about from my parents and grandparents.

I had long witnessed my parent's complete dedication to one another. Theirs still is a steady, solid love, and they've stayed committed to each other through fifty years and my mother's long battle with melanoma. My grandparents were fiercely committed to each other, too. In my Gramps, Bolton Sullivan, I saw a passionate love of his wife, literally until his death.

Gramps lived the last ten years of his life in a great deal of pain from damage to the nerve endings in his feet. He would spend hours in his chair by the window at their home in Florida and often, when I visited, he would tell me of his love for Nana. Even as he felt his body deteriorating, he repeatedly said he wanted to live because he didn't want to leave his beloved wife. Not one for sentimentality in the same way, and to diffuse the inherent sadness in what Gramps said, Nana quipped: "I'd go today if the good Lord would have me, but I'm not sure He wants a grumpy old woman like me."

By the time my grandfather was ninety-four, he had become quite frail. Nana's health had also deteriorated after she broke her hip and she developed congestive heart failure. She was sick enough that a priest was called in to bless her and read her last rites. As the priest prayed over Nana with family nearby, Gramps quietly closed his eyes in the next room and died. Incredibly sweet love. Thinking she had gone, he had clearly decided peacefully to join her; he just couldn't fathom

being separated. Just as Gramps was absolutely true to his lo
until the end, Nana was true to her loveable, cantankero
self, too: She recovered and lived many more months happi
playing bridge in a nursing home!

I hadn't yet found the man who had inspired that kind
devotion, the kind of man worthy of the kind of love I knew
was capable of giving. Honestly, I hadn't been looking t
hard. Although I hadn't experienced it yet myself, I expect
that the platitudes about true love were absolutely true.
imagined that it would involve understanding, patience, sa
rifice, selflessness, and commitment. If I was going to co
mit, I would give it my all. I wanted to pledge loyalty
another person, to a set of values, goals, and dreams, and t
family. I realize that to some this might seem the opposite
romantic. But I saw from watching and talking to my pare
that passion and romance come and go through the seas
of life; what sustains you are shared values and comm
goals. I found *that* incredibly romantic.

Just a few hours later, Mark came to the small ca
where I slept and handed me old hunting gear so we co
hike to a freshwater pond in the woods to watch the sun r
The sun was coming up as I slipped my feet into the rub
boots and donned a thread-worn jacket. Mark held my h
as we worked our way in silence to a spot in the reeds at
side of the pond where dozens of mallards and buffleh
flew in to feed. As the daylight grew brighter, I slowly bec
aware of the beauty of this place. Egrets and blue he
soared gracefully over the still water. Mark named the

The estate advisers told him he would have to sell the farm to meet the family's obligations, but Mark refused. Although he was only a young man, Mark stepped into the role of head of the family and made some difficult decisions to save the farm. He sold the herd of cattle that had grazed the land for years, and reluctantly let the seven full-time employees go. Much of the maintenance of the farm had to be deferred, unless Mark and his siblings could do it themselves. This was a painful time for the family, a time of stress and hardship when every day Mark feared that he might make a choice that would result in them losing this precious homestead. Yet he kept his vision clearly focused on what mattered to him and the family and, through his discipline and their collective effort, they managed to keep Coosaw.

When the sun was higher on the horizon, I walked with Mark back to the main house, a lovely but worn old brick structure. Though technically a plantation, in the light of day I could see why Mark and his siblings referred to Coosaw as a farm. To me the word "plantation" conjures an image of a grand old antebellum home with servants bringing trays of mint juleps to the veranda for men dressed in seersucker and women in cotton dresses. Coosaw certainly wasn't that. But it also didn't fit my Midwestern idea of a farm with rows of corn and barns and cows and chickens.

Scattered around the main house were several falling-down red-roofed barns with faded and chipped white paint. Old tractors and farm equipment in various states of disrepair dotted the landscape, along with a few small hunting cabins.

The Sanfords had a homemade fix for everything. They had replaced the rusted-out floor of a jeep with a sheet of plywood. Sure, Coosaw was tumbledown, but I was completely charmed.

We entered the incredibly comfortable and lived-in main house. The décor was tired, the upholstery faded and tattered, and generally the place was a mess, with dirty boots and shotguns heaped in the entryway and clothes drying by the fire. Mark's family and a few friends had congregated in the kitchen. Everyone was pitching in to prepare a big breakfast, swapping stories of hunts from the weekend, or catching up on each other's lives. When the meal was set out, we all paused, holding hands in a circle for the blessing. As soon as the meal was done, everyone was up, cleaning the kitchen or setting off to tackle one of the many chores that had been discussed over breakfast: tending the dikes, grading the dirt road, moving the tractor, fixing the dirt bike, or cleaning the guns.

I was put on the kitchen crew. While tidying the kitchen, surrounded by family photos of Sanfords at Coosaw or at the old home in Florida, I got the chance to chat at length with Mark's mother, Peg. She spoke of how delighted she was to have all of her children home. I was flooded with a sense of Mark, of his tight-knit family, of *Sanfordness*. Even though we came from very different backgrounds and parts of the country, it became clear to me there that we had a great number of things in common.

My big Catholic Midwestern family was, in its way, as close knit and fiercely loyal as Mark's Southern Protestant clan. I was raised in Winnetka, Illinois, a well-to-do suburb of Chicago. Both my parents grew up there as well, and my siblings and I all attended the same grade school, Saints Faith, Hope & Charity. I was the second child of five and the oldest of three girls in a row. It sure seemed that the girls dominated the Sullivan household, despite the presence of our brothers Bolton and John. (Perhaps that is just how I wistfully see it now, looking back from this world of mine that is so completely populated by men and boys.)

Our childhood was a happy one, safe and secure. We walked or rode our bikes to school, came home for lunch daily, and even in the dead of the winter, Mom routinely sent us out to play, warning us not to come in until dinner. There were always kids everywhere. In addition to my siblings, within just a few blocks we had *two* sets of nine first cousins. Our family gatherings never had fewer than twenty people and frequently as many as fifty. While I was studious and a bit shy, I was never lonely. The family just opposite our home had ten children, including the youngest one, who had bells attached to his shoes so his family could find him when he wandered away, often ending up lost in our house. I now can see this setting as wonderfully old-fashioned and simple; it was in many ways idyllic. I considered us blessed.

We Sullivans were certainly comfortable, but I never thought of us as wealthy. My great grandfather had founded the Skil Corporation, which manufactured the world's first portable circular saw, a Skilsaw. He started from nothing, raising enough money to make one Skilsaw, selling it, and raising enough to make another. Great Grandpa wasn't the one with business sense. That was my Gramps, who, as a very young man, took over the management of the company from his dad and made it into a national brand and a real business. My father's goal when he assumed a leadership role was to make the company international, which he did in the early 1960s; he then managed the company right through the tough business cycle in the late 1970s, when the company was eventually sold. Our family never wanted for anything, but Mom taught us to hunt for bargains. If we found something we liked, she often told us not to mention it to our father so he wouldn't worry about the cost, leading us to believe we had real financial concerns. (Her code to us, "DTF," meant "Don't Tell Father!") In fact, that may have been the case. Or it might have been part of Mom's strategy to raise appreciative and thrifty children.

We spent summers at the local country club or away at summer camp, and we vacationed yearly in Florida, visiting our grandparents. These were surely luxuries, but we otherwise lived modestly. Our house was not air-conditioned (not a big hardship in Chicago except for a couple of weeks in the summer). During heat waves, we would all sleep together in the screened porch. Once my little brother tried to cool down by dunking his head in the toilet!

Dad traveled often for business and usually played golf while home weekends spring through fall. He had then and still has a gentle spirit, a steady, diligent work ethic, and an excellent head for business, all qualities I now saw I used every day in my banking job. I consider my dad a man of great integrity. These were the same qualities I saw in Mark and his family throughout the weekend at Coosaw. Certainly no family is perfect—I had had many epiphanies about my own family's imperfections over the years, as surely most teenagers and young adults do, but I think I understood even then that looking for perfection in a partner was folly. Still, what I saw in the Sanfords that first weekend at Coosaw made me think that his family was close to perfection and a lot of that impression had to do with Mark and the courageous way he worked to save the family farm.

The gentle and thoughtful nature that had first drawn me to Mark seemed even more precious to me at Coosaw. The men I knew in finance bragged about the smallest triumphs. Here was a man who had, after the debilitating death of his father, done some of the hardest work of his life to save this beautiful land, yet had hardly mentioned a word of this to me during all the months I'd known him. For the first time, I started to think very seriously about this man: so different, sweet, and yet a challenge in so many ways.

TWO

SOON AFTER I RETURNED FROM SOUTH CAROLINA, MARK VISITED New York for a job interview and left flowers with my apartment doorman with a cute note asking me out for dinner that evening. Surprises can backfire! I already had dinner plans with another man that night, so Mark and I didn't connect on that visit. Thereafter, Mark became more focused in his efforts to woo me, sending regular notes and calling to pin my schedule down before he arrived in the city.

As we grew closer, I started visiting him on weekends at the University of Virginia, where he was finishing his MBA. I was touched when he asked me to be among his family when he graduated in May. As his graduation approached, we began to speak about the future. By the fall of 1988, Mark had moved to New York to work full-time in commercial real estate. The night he proposed the following spring, he made me a candlelight dinner and placed a beautiful family heirloom ring on my finger. We planned the wedding for November at my parents' place in Florida.

Although I had just been named a vice president at Lazard, a rarity for a woman in her twenties, I knew I could walk away without regret if we decided to move to South Carolina. I had pursued a job in investment banking but my long-term ambition had always been business in general. In my senior undergraduate year at Georgetown, one of my professors suggested I send a resume to Lazard, a top-drawer firm with no female partners and a notorious "sink-or-swim" mentality. I didn't think I had a chance, but I dutifully sent it off. As luck would have it, I was one of four analysts hired that year, and the only female. Shortly after graduation, I moved to New York to begin the job. I hoped to learn a great deal from it, but planned to eventually return to the Midwest for a less crazed corporate position.

Every day I walked down Fifth Avenue past the huge gleaming gold statute of Prometheus in front of 1 Rockefeller Center on my way to work. When the elevator doors opened on Lazard's headquarters, however, the atmosphere was surprisingly shabby. The carpet was soiled, and the desks were old and mismatched. These tattered conditions were part of the company's philosophy. The partners prided themselves on producing the most reliable advice, rewarding themselves handsomely with the profits and leaving little left over for decorations or the latest technology. My first office was in a small room I shared with two associates and three bulky computers. Yet despite the threadbare infrastructure, the atmosphere was electric.

I started there in the "greed is good" era of the 1980s, when huge corporations were taking over smaller companies, splitting off deadwood business interests and turning around to combine forces again and again. Lazard was in the thick of everything. My job in mergers and acquisitions was to help with the process of valuing the companies to be acquired, merged, or sold. I worked with an intensity that amazes me now.

As a deal was coming together, the partner in charge had his team of associates scrambling. Though market conditions seemed favorable at that moment, we all knew that opportunities could disappear in a flash, taking fortunes with them. We had to get our part exactly right. If just one number was off, millions could be lost. Partners shared in the enormous profits of the firm, an incredible motivation for them and all the ambitious young people, like me, who crunched numbers long into the night and through most every weekend. Too many mornings I went home only to shower and change my clothes before heading back.

One winter afternoon in the early months of my time at Lazard, I was in the company library searching for documents. I heard a loud whoosh and jerked my head up from the files to see a dark blur streak past the library window. I pressed my face to the window to see what had just fallen and trembled when I saw a figure imprinted on the roof of a car. Later I found out that this was a stock trader who had jumped out the window of the floor directly above me. I cried and shook again when I learned he had left behind a wife and young family.

Often in the years that followed while I worked at Lazard, I would think of that dark imprint far below and speculate about what had driven the man to jump. Was it some personal demon? Or was it this life all of us were leading? This work demanded everything you had. We lived on a scale and at a pace where few could survive for long. Looking at some of the partners, I could see how the endless pursuit of today's opportunity throws life off balance. In time, the same thing began to happen to me. I was burning out.

It wasn't a straight line from seeing that suicide to changing the pace of my own life, but a few years after the death of that trader, despite promotions and solidly increasing pay for my work, I asked to be re-assigned to a job with steadier hours for a year. The powers that be agreed it was time for me to broaden my knowledge of the business, so they moved me to the bond desk in capital markets. The new assignment was dull by comparison and didn't use the best of my skills, but I was happy because the new schedule was predictable. I could make plans—and keep them! I could see more of my friends and have good visits with my family. And it was during this time that I met Mark.

There is a chance that if he had crossed my path a few months earlier, I wouldn't have noticed the charm of that soft-spoken Southerner. The fact that I was not driving myself so hard gave me the biggest luxury of all: time. With more time on my hands, I was noticing different things, or at least I had more time to consider what I was really seeing. I looked up from my frenzy and there was Mark, humble, hardworking, whip smart, stunningly handsome, with a clever but subtle sense of humor.

Before we were engaged, I returned to the banking side of things. One night while eating take-out food over work at the office, a manila envelope arrived at my desk via courier. I opened it to find a formal legal document with a handwritten note from Mark attached by a paper clip. "Dearest Jenny, I know we haven't discussed this so why don't you just sign the attached and return to me and we can move quietly on from here."

The document looked legitimate; I began to fume as I read:

> "This **PRENUPTIAL AGREEMENT** is made this ___ day of May, 1989, between the undersigned parties, Jennifer C. Sullivan (hereinafter referred to as "Wife"), of New York, New York, and Marshall C. Sanford, Jr. (hereinafter referred to as "Husband") of Dale, South Carolina.
>
> **WHEREAS,** both parties are above the age of eighteen (18) years and, notwithstanding the sagacious counsel of their parents, peers and true inner selves, wish to become husband and wife; and
>
> **WHEREAS,** both parties wish to establish an efficient mechanism for resolving the innumerable dif-

ferences which they anticipate will arise throughout their married lives; and

WHEREAS, the parties desire to set forth their agreements and understandings herein;

NOW, THEREFORE, in consideration of the foregoing, of the mutual promises herein set forth, of the invaluable loss of personal freedom and dignity, and of other good and sufficient consideration, the receipt of which is hereby acknowledged, the parties agree as follows:

1. **Purposes.** The purpose of this marriage are manifolded to provide companionship during two drab and uneventful lives; to pool resources in order to forestall the inevitable effects of an erratic and ruinous economy; to provide a convenient source of blame for whatever tragedies, short of nuclear attack, befall the parties together or individually; and not incidentally, to vent either party's wanton, shameful and animalistic desires.

2. **Term.** The marriage shall be solemnified on November 4, 1989, and shall seem to last a lifetime whether it does or not.

In skimming those first clauses it dawned on me that this must be a joke. But as I read on, I wasn't so sure because there were shades of the Mark I knew in the demands he was making. Still, I hoped he was poking fun at himself.

> 3. **Expenses.** Wife agrees to share equally the expenses of maintaining the household. Additionally, Wife agrees to limit her expenditures for all her personal items and usages (including but not limited to, clothes, panty hose, make-up, jewelry, perfume, automobiles, entertainment, medical bills and medicines) to ONE HUNDRED DOLLARS ($100) per month, which amount may be increased only by the written agreement of parties. Any amount not spent in any given month shall lapse.
>
> 4. **Decisions.** The parties recognize that numerous decisions must be made each day which affect the parties together or individually, and recognize, too, the necessity for a decisionmaker in the event of their inability to agree on the proper solution to any particular problem. In deference to Husband's gender-related superior intellect and judgment, Wife hereby agrees that Husband will be the final arbiter in all matters. . . .

"Gender-related superior intellect" must have been the tip-off for me. I was laughing out loud when I called Mark to "thank" him for the thoughtful "delivery." I was impressed with the time and creativity he had put into this hoax. He had pulled a fast one on me, a hard person to fool. This fake prenup was filled with outlandish things a chauvinistic, selfish, and single-minded husband might desire of a wife and

Mark was none of those things. Today I do wonder at some of the clauses that have proven true over time, despite the fact that we never signed the silly thing. Mark is notoriously frugal so his fake demands about spending and accountability foreshadowed one aspect of our life together. But it is Clause 9, having to do with children, that I find most prescient: "In the event of pregnancy, Wife hereby agrees to make male children." I couldn't have known then that I would have only sons, even if I did learn that it was one of Mark's dearest wishes that he have them.

Every individual within a couple brings differences of perspective and experience to a marriage, and Mark and I were no different in that regard. Whereas I tend to trust in what the future will bring and live very much in the here and now, Mark needs goals to focus his future and by which he can assess his progress. Once during our engagement he asked me to meet him at a restaurant for dinner and told me to bring a list of my lifetime goals for us to discuss. I chuckled when I saw he had brought a notepad with pages of goals, dreams, and hoped-for adventures. I carried a blank piece of paper. He was astonished at what he took to be my lack of ambitions, but I explained that my goals were pretty straightforward and writing them down wouldn't clarify them for me. I had thought long and hard about his request. In the end, I really only wanted to be remembered as a good mother and grandmother; a life well-lived by me would leave behind generations of well-adjusted and happy children, each productive in their own way.

Needless to say our conversation continued for a very long while that evening and, in fact, it was a conversation we revisited almost annually for many years to come. Once encouraged to put pencil to paper, my list grew and included becoming involved in something I considered a worthy cause (as opposed to making money just for the sake of it), running my own business one day, and being a good wife to Mark. Also, because I was determined to get good enough to keep up with Mark and the other Sanfords, I added that I wanted to learn to hunt and be able to shoot just one quail in my lifetime.

To be fair, I admired that Mark had thought so seriously and carefully about the benchmarks of his success, but I can see now that this was an early inkling of an aspect of his character that was just under his gentle, thoughtful manner: his profound restlessness.

Mark's goals were divided into several categories including physical, career, financial, mental, spiritual, family, and values. On his "physical" list were the goals to climb Mt. Rainier, bike across America, and consistently beat his brothers in tennis. He also wanted to take an "adventure" trip annually. For his career and financial goals, he set the bar high as well: He wanted to be an articulate spokesman and motivator of men, make a good deal of money, and own his own company by the time he was 30, and he aspired to one day be a U.S. Senator. I couldn't argue with his ambition and I loved his many ideas for adventure travel. Later Mark would keep an adventure resume in addition to a work resume; seeing the exotic and far-flung corners of the world has provided us both with many wonderful memories and experiences, though because of our children, it was often Mark who traveled on these adventures alone.

He even had spiritual goals. He shaped those by memorizing and aspiring to "live by" Bible verses that best encapsulated his thinking. He cherished Galatians 5:22: "The fruit of the Spirit is love, joy, peace, patience, kindness, goodness, faithfulness, gentleness and self-control." He also wanted to follow Matthew 5:16: "Let your light so shine before men, that they may see your good works and praise your Father in heaven."

Faith has been a constant in my life ever since I was a small child comforted by watching my parents pray, saying blessings at meals, and being tucked into bed with a prayer. Faith in our extended family wasn't just something you had, it was something you lived. I saw my dad pray nightly on his knees before his cross. Though he rarely preached to us, when I saw my father, such a huge figure to me, praying in this humble position, I felt the serenity of knowing that someone was always watching from above. Sunday mass at the Catholic church down the street was an unquestioned part of the family routine, and for my parents, it was often a daily practice. Faith and family was a constant mix and a steady presence.

While I had learned all about the Bible in church and school, we were never taught to commit a verse to memory. I was impressed at how lightly these powerful words tripped off Mark's tongue. He knew these verses so well that they had become part of how he saw the world. When I got home, I looked them up so that I could think more about what Mark wanted to "personify and live." The more I thought about these, the more I agreed that they described worthy spiritual goals, albeit coming at me in an unfamiliar way.

Although Mark's family and mine worshipped in different ways, I believed we shared the same values. Mark reinforced this in my mind when he agreed that we could do our religious preparation for marriage in the Catholic church I was attending in New York City. A very close friend of my family's was a Jesuit priest, Fr. Leo O'Donovan, and he agreed, after meeting Mark and thoroughly discussing his faith, to marry us in a Catholic ceremony in a nondenominational church. Nothing about this in any way felt like relinquishing my own faith. Mark and I were bringing our respective traditions together and the blend seemed then—and turned out to remain—effortless.

A short while before the wedding, when Mark and I were picking readings and vows, Mark told me that he didn't want to use a wedding vow that included the promise to be faithful. He was worried in some odd nagging way, he said, that he might not be able to remain true to that vow. In retrospect, I suppose I might have seen this as a sign that Mark wasn't fully committed to me, and with the benefit of the knowledge I have about Mark now, I could point to this moment as a clear sign of things to come.

At the time, though, I thought his honesty was brave and sweet, and I suppose I also thought it was a classic case of pre-wedding cold feet. But I took his concern seriously. I told him that I had unshakable faith in him and thought that his values and moral principles matched up—and would continue to match up—with his actions in the world. As often as I have replayed this moment from our young relationship in my memory, I can't see it any other way. Being unfaithful was not inevitable. I know that many men doubt that they can remain faithful to their wives for life, but I believed that Mark was among those who would be able to do so.

Nonetheless, he had raised the issue and we needed to talk it through. I explained to Mark that I believed marriage was so much more than words spoken in a vow and that I was marrying him because I was deeply in love with him as a whole and even flawed human being. More than that, it seemed fundamental to a happy marriage that one would have a partner who had unwavering faith in you and thought better of you than you thought of yourself. To me marriage was a lifetime commitment made to one another in front of God, family, and friends. The specifics of what we *said* weren't important to me, but rather the spirit of the ceremony. And I pointed out that fidelity was implied no matter how we phrased it—it was one of the fundamental commandments!

I tried to explain to Mark that I felt that marriage was in many ways a leap of faith. I put my faith in his goodness more than anything else, and he needed to do the same with me. We would be two people holding hands and leaping into an uncertain future. How could we know what that future would hold for us? We had to trust that we could make it together no matter what fate threw our way. So long as our commitment remained our priority, I told him I knew we could weather any storm. I can see now how this might sound like I was *convincing* Mark to be faithful to me, but that's not how the conversation unfolded. Instead, my clear conviction about what marriage meant and my faith in his ability to live up to it seemed to calm him. He said he wholeheartedly agreed.

In Fr. Leo's homily at the ceremony he spoke of the privilege family and friends felt to be present as "You begin the journey of lives shared together completely. Perhaps the notion of journey, or pilgrimage, is as fitting an image as we can find for human life in general—and certainly for marriage." He also said, "I can promise you that what you will discover about each other will amaze and comfort and, yes, perhaps occasionally trouble you. The joy of it is that you set off on the journey together. . . . Jesus is united to us as a symbol of God's everlasting covenant, and the marriage of this young man and woman symbolizes that union for us. It is in each other's faces that they will see God and show God to us. It is in their goodness to the men and women around them, but above all in their goodness to each other that they will learn how the love of neighbor is indeed a single commandment with the love of God." He concluded, "If you ever doubt that you are the face of God for each other, remember that we today, with enormous joy and confidence, see God radiant in both of you."

THREE

I CAN ONLY BEST DESCRIBE OUR NEWLY MARRIED LIFE AS BLISSFUL. We were young and healthy (or soon to be in his case—he battled a serious case of mono when we returned from our honeymoon and for many weeks he could do little more than sleep). We were deeply in love and had a world of possibilities in front of us both. We were beginning the satisfying and happy work of building a life together.

Mark moved into my Manhattan apartment and I continued working while he tried to get a new real estate company off the ground, one with a goal of investing in properties in the Southeast. I knew his heart wouldn't stay engaged in New York City living as long as his focus continued to point south, and I knew all along that a move was in order.

During one of Mark's business trips south, he found an

historic house—called a tenement because it shared a wall with the house next door—on Wentworth Street, in downtown Charleston. It had lost its roof in the big hurricane of 1989, Hugo. The extensive repairs the house needed made it affordable for us, and it was in the heart of Charleston, which promised activity for me and an office for Mark within walking distance of our home. Another advantage was that we would be only about an hour from Coosaw.

I can still remember seeing the house for the first time. Even in all its disrepair, it was charming; it would be ours. The original builder had brought his maritime experience to bear on the entrance: The entrances to both sides of the building were flanked with lights—red and green—like the ones marking the channel into the Charleston harbor. The exterior was old brick and the inside had high ceilings and random-width heart-of-pine floors, quite common in old Charleston homes, but exotic to me at the time.

From New York we supervised repairs to make the home safe and comfortable. Mark hired an old friend who was a contractor to put up new Sheetrock on the damaged walls and replace broken glass, as well as make some minor upgrades in the kitchen and bathrooms. Mark questioned his friend about every expenditure and negotiated ways to bring the work in at the price he wanted to pay. Miraculously, everything got done without them coming to blows.

Although we were both committed to this move, when we talked about Charleston, Mark worried out loud that I would miss the fast pace of the big city.

I knew he was wrong about that. Truth be told I could hardly wait to begin our life there.

As it happened, on one of my last days at Lazard, I shared an elevator with the formidable head of the firm, Michel David-Weill, a diminutive man who reportedly earned about $50 million each year. Ruddy-faced and white-haired, Michel looked up at me over his spectacles and asked in his thick French accent, "But Jen-ni-fer, what weel you do in zeez South Caroliiiina? Who weel you talk to?"

I didn't worry about having people to talk with. South Carolina had a tremendous amount to offer and fascinating people. I hoped we would be blessed with children, and I knew that investment banking did not mix well with having a family. Michel was right about one thing, though. I would need to keep my mind busy and remain involved in something that would balance time with the kids, should we be lucky enough to have them. But beyond that, I knew I wanted to be home for our children as much as I could be while they were young. I had no confidence whatsoever that I would get the child-rearing right. Time would be the judge of that. I did know that I had only one real chance—while they were young—to make a mark on their lives and I took that seriously.

Before we moved to Charleston in early December we had the old floors refinished. The weather was so damp, however, that the floors took longer than expected to dry. We redirected the moving truck to Coosaw for an extra few days. Mark convinced the drivers not to charge us for the delay in exchange for giving them a cabin to stay in at Coosaw and plenty of time to spend with a gun in a deer stand. There is no doubt a lot of backroom negotiating and compromise involved in getting things done in New York and in many other places in this country, too, but this particular barter system—move us in tomorrow and welcome yourself to some hunting on my land while you wait—struck me as wonderfully southern.

Of course, there were many "we're not in Kansas anymore, Toto" moments in those early days in Charleston. Ever used to walking briskly down New York City's streets with my eyes down, tightly clutching my purse, I loved the pleasant greetings we received from strangers as we walked the streets of this genteel and more relaxed city, my purse swinging freely and my head and shoulders focused happily ahead.

Homemaking was also a revelation. Mark and I decided we could make the cosmetic improvements on the house ourselves. I painted some of the rooms and the kitchen floor, made curtains, and even learned to hang wallpaper by myself. We didn't have a dining table, so Mark dragged a musty drop-leaf one out of the barn at Coosaw, along with a few old chairs, which I cleaned and then covered with fresh fabric. He also found a set of twin beds for the guest bedroom that I painted so they wouldn't look so dingy. There was no telling what had lived in the mattresses he found in the barn to put on those beds, but we used them anyway.

It was in living together in a space new to both of us—sharing my apartment had still been sharing *my* apartment—

that we began to rub up against each other and start to work out a complementary way to be. Living together for the first time was one thing: Getting used to someone's habits and quirks can test your patience. But for us, it was the traditions and expectations that we had each inherited from our families that started to highlight our differences. I know this is common—I think I must have known this even then—and see now that this is the real task of the beginning of a shared life. Discovering these things about another person and learning to love and honor the differences were our next tasks.

While living in our house on Wentworth, however, I quickly learned firsthand of Mark's frugality and how it would now impact my every move. After getting a South Carolina driver's license, I wanted a car so I would not have to depend on Mark if I needed to go somewhere outside the neighborhood. He was against buying a new car so he went with his friend Ozzie, a used-car dealer, to an auction to make sure he got the most for his money. I didn't gripe—I needed a mode of transportation, not a seat of luxury—but Mark's frugality quickly showed itself to be his badge of honor and something I had to get used to.

As careful as he was with our money, however, it was a little ironic that he wasn't terrific at keeping track of things, at least in any way that another person could make sense of. Mark wrote down on scraps of paper important transactions such as swapping a tract of land with one of his brothers. Later, even though he remembered to the letter the deal they'd made, he'd struggle to find the note that backed it up.

It wasn't long before I took over the family checkbook. Mark agreed happily because he knew that I could tend to the minutiae, but would always keep him informed of the bigger picture. I made a balance sheet with our overall financial position, marital assets combined, and he seemed to breathe easier. Still he wanted to watch and approve every dime I spent, which drove me mad. Eventually I learned we could peacefully coexist if I kept overall expenses to an agreed-upon level, but was free to choose where to save or to spend. This arrangement helped us both avoid petty disagreements.

Little did I realize as a young woman in love that there would be many moments when these same qualities, particularly his frugality, would cost me. I remember the first birthday I celebrated after we moved south. Mark gave me a hand-made birthday card with a picture of him holding birthday balloons on the front. I thought it was sweet that he drew a picture for me himself. But inside the card, strangely, was a picture of half a bike. I didn't quite understand the picture. Mark explained I would get the other half in the future. Well, that Christmas he drew me a picture of the other half of the bike, and months later, he delivered the gift to me, a used purple bike he had purchased for $25! My reaction at first was disbelief; he had given me nicer gifts while engaged. In time, however, I came to know this was just part of who he was. And I could play along: A few years ago, we were trying to put aside some money for repairs on a small cottage at Coosaw, so for Christmas I drew Mark a picture of half a house!

In addition to the more common compromises on finances and blending our faith traditions, our marriage brought unexpected challenges as I grew to know more deeply what made Mark tick. If one of the primary tasks in a young marriage is for both of the new partners to separate completely from their families so that they can form traditions of their own, that first Thanksgiving, less than four weeks into our married life, I saw how difficult that task would be for Mark.

When all of the Sanford siblings arrived at the farm for the holiday weekend, Mark promptly took our bags upstairs where there are two bedrooms and one shared bathroom. Mark's mother's bedroom was on the first floor and traditionally one of the rooms upstairs had always been his sister Sarah's. The other large bedroom (with bunk beds, trundles, desks, and even surfboards hanging from the ceiling) was for Mark and his brothers. I was confused. Were we displacing Sarah? I thought surely we'd be sleeping in one of the small cabins, perhaps even the one I'd stayed in alone when I first came here for New Year's Eve. Instead, Mark explained, I would be sleeping with his sister while he slept across the hall with his brothers.

"You've got to be kidding!" I said.

"I've always slept with my brothers and I don't see why that has to change now that we're married," he replied matter-of-factly. This was no big deal for him—it just was what it was. I thought it was absurd. In the end, we didn't have to stand in that hall (that oddly doubles as a closet) disagreeing for long. Mark had just been diagnosed with mono and that made him an undesirable bunkmate. His brothers voted him out. We stayed in one of the small cottages after all.

It was also in our first year of our marriage that my sweet grandfather closed his eyes, thinking he was off to join his wife, who he was sure had died in the next room. When the news of his death came to me I relayed it tearfully to Mark and told him I'd set about making reservations for us to fly to Chicago for the funeral. Mark, however, said he wouldn't be going. He explained that he had hardly known my grandfather. Having only met him a handful of times, he didn't think he needed to be at the funeral.

I was hurt, even angry, and I cried then for both my grandfather and Mark's lack of sensitivity. This seemed so out of character for his thoughtful and gentle nature. I explained that I wanted Mark to travel to Chicago to support me in mourning for a person I had adored. I explained how it was something I needed, and that it was expected of him; my family might also feel hurt by his absence. But Mark held firm that he didn't need to go with me to the funeral.

Somewhere in the tears (mine) and the stoicism (his), I realized that Mark and I had never talked about funerals in relation to our respective faiths and traditions. I took a deep breath and asked Mark to tell me of the services he had been to in his life and to describe what funerals meant to him. I learned then that Mark had only been to one funeral in his life: his father's.

Dr. Sanford had died surrounded by his family on

Thanksgiving Day in 1982. Mark and a family friend built a cypress casket, and then brothers Billy and John dug a deep grave beneath their Dad's favorite oak tree with a backhoe. After a service at church in Beaufort the family drove to the gravesite on Coosaw with a very small group of friends. There was a short burial blessing and then the few guests and Peg departed, followed by Sarah, who wanted to walk home alone along the river. Then Mark and his brothers used three shovels to carefully cover their Dad's coffin with dirt, working until the top was made smooth and neat again. This was his experience with the end of life and with marking someone's passing. It started to make sense to me that he didn't feel it would be appropriate to be part of the service for my grandfather. To him, a funeral was a deeply personal and private affair. My pleading and my explanation that my tradition was very different—my grandfather's funeral would be a big Irish Catholic Celebration of Life—didn't change Mark's mind. I traveled to Chicago alone.

As disappointing as it was to not have Mark's support, learning the full story of his father's funeral helped me understand my husband better. A father's death is a huge event in any life, but Mark's father's was extraordinary in the way it shaped Mark's worldview.

When his father fell ill, Mark felt responsible to his father and his family. In a way, from the moment that his father was diagnosed, Mark's youth ended. After his father died, the tough decisions Mark had to make to save Coosaw made him the embodiment of someone who had lived through an experience like the Great Depression, almost like someone from another time. This was at the heart of his deep-seated frugality and his constant sense of his own mortality. I knew he would always wonder what he missed out on in life because of taking on so much at a young age.

In understanding this, I learned not to take personally Mark's thrifty ways, but I also started to appreciate in a deeper way the different loads we each carried into our shared emotional space. It became clear why Mark had asked me to have that discussion about goals, and why his many different goals had to be listed on pages and pages. He needed to accomplish as much as he could in whatever time God granted him. This also helps explain why Mark could be restless and impulsive.

After we finished renovating our house, Mark began agitating for the next big project. Our house came with an adjacent vacant lot. After less than a year, we sold the house we renovated and rented a house nearby so that we could design and build a new home on that vacant lot. We wanted our new home to be one we would own forever and yet one that was uncomplicated and easy to leave for weekends spent at Coosaw or for longer breaks in the summer. City living was fine for Mark, but he was adamant that he never wanted to feel closed in, so we made having a view of the harbor an important part of the design.

Building a house from the ground up is exhilarating. You watch your ideas, your creation, your hopes and dreams start to blossom with each new wall put up and floor laid down. But I don't recommend it for the faint of heart. Even the best of teams have faltered under the pressure of so many large and so many petty decisions. And the way money seems to hemorrhage, even the most careful accounting can make your head spin.

I had, of course, learned with our first home renovation how important sticking to a budget was for Mark. I also learned how much I disliked having his fingers in every little decision I made. Unless we divided our areas of decision making, I knew we'd end up arguing about the cost of doorknobs, and I didn't want him micromanaging the nonfinancial decisions such as paint color either. We avoided conflict in our second home the same way we had over our checkbook. We came up with an overall budget and design for the house and then split responsibilities, with each of us having complete control of specific areas with attached budgets.

Mark dealt with the outside of the house and the garage, yard, roof, and deck, while I dealt with all details of the interior. If I wanted expensive curtains, then I would need to skimp on cabinets or vice versa. I trusted him with the choice of brick or with shutters and he trusted my choice of paint colors and fabrics, all within the original boundaries we had agreed to. This turned out to be an incredibly effective way to survive the project, and I'm not a little proud to be able to look back at that time and see that two controlling personalities (one who was also a penny-pincher, and the other who realized she was pregnant) worked as a real team through it all.

Yes, too true. Shortly after settling into the rental home I discovered I was pregnant. This was a real surprise to both of us; starting a family was a few years off on both of our lists of goals. I was immediately excited nonetheless. Mark, however, was quite anxious at first. He thought he would be better suited to be a father if he was a bit older (his father was 45 when Mark was born) and he worried too what he would do, how he would react, the way he would play and interact, if this baby was a girl. At first his mumblings seemed funny. I couldn't quite believe that the idea of a baby girl would cause him so much fear. But I soon realized that his anxiety was real. Even as he started to get excited about the idea of a baby—and he did; we both embraced it pretty quickly—he imagined boys, sons. His sister was always "one of the boys" in his childhood household. I often think that a girl would have been great for Mark. She might have softened him up a bit, and I know he would have been a wonderful father to her. But somehow God gives you only what you can handle. Maybe sons are what Mark could handle. Little did either of us know there would be four!

Mark and I worked together on plans for the new house and then watched it being built as my belly grew. Friends held a baby shower for me, and I prepared a small nursery in the house while Mark continued to keep his fingers crossed for a boy. I was able to continue playing golf and tennis and even worked planting fields at Coosaw while pregnant, though I did tire more easily as I grew quite large. Mark joined me at one Lamaze class before deeming it a waste of his time since, as he explained, "I've spent many long nights helping cows give birth and I know what to do when the baby gets stuck." Of course, many fathers still didn't attend births in those days, so Mark didn't really feel he needed to know too much about the human birthing process. Instead, my sister Kathy came to be with me for the birth. We spent lots of time taking bike rides on the cobblestone streets in Charleston hoping to help nudge delivery along, to no avail.

When I was almost two weeks overdue, my labor was induced. Delivered at 10 pounds, 5 ounces, on June 23, our first son, Marshall, was a healthy, very content baby whom Mark delightfully began to refer to as the "little man." Mark was instantly a very proud and very doting father. He called his family and mine to brag of this fine baby boy and to tell them all how healthy and handsome he was. Mark's mother, Peg, came to stay with us for a few days and I was thankful for the help since I was not all that nimble after the delivery.

Mark's enthusiasm for Marshall was wonderful to witness, but I could see changing diapers would not be his strong suit. He had planned a trip to climb Mt. Rainier with a few friends and, as the baby had been late in coming, his trip would begin when Marshall was only two weeks old. Marshall took to nursing right away, and he usually slept well between feedings. I was comfortable and confident in my mothering instincts. I didn't really see any reason for Mark not to go off and enjoy his adventure.

Actually, taking care of a newborn alone while Mark traveled turned out to be much easier in many ways than assimilating to life at Coosaw with Mark and his siblings while raising Marshall.

I remember waking up with Marshall as the sun rose one morning on a family-filled holiday weekend and having a difficult time keeping him safe in the kitchen while I heated his bottle. He was crawling around the floor, which was, as usual, littered with farm dirt and dead cockroaches, and I saw scattered shotgun shells too. If that wasn't enough, that morning there were also beer bottles left by Mark's younger siblings who had likely gone to bed just hours before. I happen to love the abandon with which the Sanfords look at cleanliness at Coosaw, but throwing a baby into the mix and then adding his siblings and their habits made it all quite a challenge at times.

Pulling a shotgun shell from my baby's tight grasp was all the more ironic given my mother's involvement in gun control. Mom has long had a can-do attitude, and when I was about eight, she became particularly frustrated reading about so many shooting deaths in Chicago. She decided to do something about it and worked with a few fellow moms to create an organization that soon became one of the first national efforts toward handgun control. They started a campaign to "Ban the Bullet" with slogans like "We need guns like we need a hole in the head!"

This brought her all sorts of good attention and some unwelcome as well. We had to unlist our home phone number due to the many threats we received from outraged gun owners, and a national hardware store chain even refused to do business with Skil as a result of mom's gun-control lobby. She was invited to appear on the *Today* show in the early 1970s, and my sister Gier and I were lucky enough to travel with her to New York. I remember being excited about flying to the big city for the first time, staying in a hotel, and eating at a fancy restaurant, not the important work our mother was doing there.

I now fully understand the many people—in South Carolina and elsewhere—who take seriously the right to bear arms, but remain amazed that my mom's gun-control efforts were not brought to light and used against Mark in our campaigns. I also remain amazed that our babies survived those early days pioneering at Coosaw.

FOUR

By fall of 1992 I was enchanted with the newfound joys of motherhood and enjoying every minute of life in this historic, eclectic, and sophisticated little town. We had a beautiful baby, were building a dream house, and shared an exquisite farm nearby. Also, I had developed many new and dear friendships with such women as Virginia Lane, an architect down the street, and Sally Coen, then my across-the-street neighbor, who had recently had her first son, too. I had also become close with Lalla Lee Campsen, who wasn't anything like my traditionally Irish Catholic New York and Chicago friends. Lalla Lee is sweet and very Southern, and she is a great shot, drives a boat well, and doesn't drink. Lalla Lee's family has a hunting spot near Coosaw, and she and her husband Chip met through Mark. Together she and I shared time outdoors with our boys and our tennis games, but we also shared our spiritual sides.

With good girlfriends to complete the picture, Mark and I had such a wonderful quality of life, unlike anything I had experienced while in New York. We had enough money, but this wasn't about riches. For lack of a better way to say it, I was so *pleased* by all Mark and I had accomplished in the few years we had been married. I knew every compromise I'd made to bring this about had been wise and I didn't think of any of the choices I had made as sacrifices. For all of the pieces of my identity—my work, most importantly—and my family traditions that I'd surrendered, I'd received blessings that were so much stronger and more precious to me: my husband, our child, our home, and our rich life in Charleston.

Mark and I were smiling one hot, sticky evening as we watched Marshall sleeping peacefully in his crib when Mark said, "Jenny, with the exception of that little man, I'm bored with life. I want to be stretched and pushed to the point of exhaustion. I want to be consumed. I don't want to just exist."

A little taken aback, I noted that this was ironic, since he had been so concerned about whether I would be bored when we moved here. It now seemed our roles were reversed. He acknowledged this irony, but he brushed it aside. His restlessness was awake again and apparent on his face.

I understood Mark's need to travel and to seek adventure, and all along I encouraged that, while hoping he would find what he needed to settle his spirit. Now, as his wife, I sensed his frustration and shared it in a way, absorbing what I could for him but unable to cure whatever it was that lay at the heart of his angst.

Shortly after announcing the need for something new to do, Mark considered some more significant real estate ventures, and his angst began to take a more specific direction. As he looked at the local and regional markets and the economy, he also considered the national climate that affected his ability to accomplish his goals. This was during Bill Clinton's first administration, and Mark began to worry about the big-spending ways of our federal government and what that meant for our young and growing family if spending was not brought under control. On many occasions, we talked at length and deeply about his frustrations. As a way to focus his thinking, he wrote a thirty-page paper on the national debt and the problems with our Social Security system. I engaged in the policy talk over countless dinners, though I have to admit that the paper made my eyes glaze over. What was exciting, however, was that it ignited a passion in Mark, and I was happy to see him energized and focused.

Mark began to pay attention when the congressional seat for our coastal district, which runs from just south of Charleston up the coast to the North Carolina border, opened up when the incumbent retired. The race for the seat had already attracted a number of people who were actively campaigning. There were two well-financed candidates running (the favorite, Van Hipp, had run the state Republican Party) and a third who had very high name recognition because his father, who had the same name, was a long-time Congressman for the district in years prior. Mark met with local business and political leaders to discuss what they wanted from the next person who would represent that district in Congress. I saw how interested Mark was in getting the right person in that position, but I didn't think he imagined *he* might be the right person. Aside from Mark's exploring candidate positions, we had talked very little of party politics. In South Carolina, you don't register to vote with a party affiliation, so I actually had to ask Mark which party he considered himself to be a part of. While unwavering in his conservative principles, he considered his answer before declaring he was a Republican.

While Mark was pondering deficits and Social Security, I found myself pregnant again. This time, neither of us was much surprised. We both wanted several children and had wasted no time working toward that goal after Marshall was born. Soon after settling into our new house, we welcomed our next son. My labor was induced before the due date because Marshall had been so big. On September 28, 1993, John Landon was born easily, weighing in at a mild 7 pounds, 10 ounces. Mark was wild with joy at having a second son. He was tender and sweet with both Marshall and Landon from the very first moment he held them. As one of my favorite Psalms, Psalm 127, puts it: "Like arrows in the hands of a fighting man are sons born to a man in his youth. Happy is he who has his quiver full." Mark was well on his way to enjoying a quiver full.

Still, he was restless.

I was in the hospital recovering from Landon's delivery when Mark formalized something that by then I'd known he was seriously considering. He announced he'd decided to run for Congress. He said that the decision felt right and that he felt compelled to run in this particular race. Then, he dropped another bombshell:

"And, Jenny, you are going to run my campaign."

"Me? You have got to be kidding! I've never even volunteered on anyone's campaign!"

"But you're free," he continued.

"Free? I think my plate is pretty full right now!" I said. I was still in the hospital bed, after all. Clearly he meant a different kind of free.

"You can do this with the babies at home," he explained "and we can just put a phone line in the kitchen. The only way this will even possibly work is if we keep our expenses incredibly low and that's why I really need you. You are free. I know why I am running and have my ideas all mapped out but I need someone to keep the trains running on time, and you are great with that kind of stuff."

I wish I could say that I threw my head back and laughed at Mark's logic or that I was wildly enthusiastic at the prospect of working hard for no pay. Instead, my honest reaction was that Mark had devised a plan that was textbook blind leading the blind. But I did know a sparkle in Mark's eye when I saw one. This decision might be the thing that would still his restlessness. Even though this work was really about achieving Mark's dream and not my own, I felt it was worthy and I thought it would be something we could do together while raising our family in the midst of it all. I think I waited until I was home from the hospital with Landon, but I accepted Mark's challenge. I signed on to help him to achieve a goal. I was excited, and at the time it didn't seem like much of a sacrifice.

I suppose you could say that women are built for sacrifice. After all, we "sacrifice" a youthful, firm body to childbearing. Imagining holding that sweet baby in your arms can make the discomforts of pregnancy endurable. Over the nine months of sharing space with a growing child, a woman can find the joy that comes from physical generosity. As the baby grows, you give him life, your life: nutrients, oxygen, protection and, bit by bit, your heart. Then you launch him into the world and experience a wrenching release—emotional and physical to be sure—and then the joy that this new little person brings to you and all around you. You'd give anything to keep that child safe and to make his life good. Sacrifice? By any definition, it becomes a part of everyday life.

When Mark announced his candidacy on November 16, 1993, shortly after Landon was born, he said, "I am running because I believe that unless we do something about the debt and the deficit, it has the capacity to undermine the financial foundation on which all of our businesses, jobs, and savings rest." The local paper noted the next day that "[Sanford] has no previous experience in elected office, no name recognition and little backing" (*Post and Courier*, November 17, 1993). The paper continued, "'What's wrong with regular folks who don't have name recognition going out and getting involved in politics?' he [Mark] asked. Will it work? Not too often in South Carolina politics will an unknown step in and win a race for Congress."

I told Mark that I would put all my efforts toward helping him get elected this one time, but if he did not win, I was not willing to do it again and again as so many others seem to do. One shot. Thus I agreed, quite naïvely, to run Mark's race for U.S. Congress. Never once, to my recollection, did either one of us question or discuss what would happen if he were to win.

FIVE

As a child in Chicago, we Sullivans were fans of the Cubs, but when push came to shove, we were Braves fans through and through. My father, mom's brother (my Uncle Tom), and a few of their friends owned the Milwaukee Braves long before owning baseball teams was profitable. When the team became the Atlanta Braves and even after the team was sold, we continued to think of them as our home team; we cheered for them over the Cubs any time they were in town.

We Sullivans also, of course, had brand loyalty to Skil products. We steered clear of all things Black & Decker.

As I got older, I understood loyalty to be the intangible thing on display between siblings and cousins—I had so many living nearby that it seemed we were one big mutual fan club. What an incredible gift it was to have such a supportive family clan, a ready and reliable cheering squad for any and all of us. I think I also understood that loyalty was at the root of good marriages. I could see that my parents were unfailingly loyal to one another, as were both sets of grandparents. This was not blind loyalty, but the kind of support that comes from knowing another person deeply, having committed to helping them succeed in life, and loving them warts and all.

It was not until Mark decided to enter politics, however, that I felt profound loyalty in my own bones and recognized it would be essential to our marriage and our goals.

That first intense congressional campaign was such an uphill challenge that it seemed to others, and sometimes to me, that the effort was hopeless, a pointless quest that could never end in victory. In many ways, the hopelessness of his quest was irrelevant to him. Mark was an ideologue with strong beliefs and a sense of urgency for change that would not be stilled. He saw this run at government office as a chance to inform others of the risks of debt and deficits. Whether he won or not, he hoped to change the public discourse on these issues. This, he felt, was an undertaking that would satisfy his need to be challenged intellectually and that would give him the exhausted thrill that comes with a job well done and a battle well fought. Simply put: The prospect of running a different kind of campaign, one based on principles and values, energized him. When Mark put his real estate business in the hands of a partner so he could focus full-time on the campaign, I knew he was serious.

Mark and I understood that as a complete political unknown, he would have trouble raising money. To get started, however, we needed some base capital. We decided to loan our campaign $100,000 of our own money—money we had earned and saved and some I had inherited—so we could compete with the better-financed opponents.

Our strategy was to raise as much money as possible and spend very little of it until the end of the race when most regular folks were deciding who would get their votes. Our first big expense was campaign stationery, which we used to write to anyone we had ever known asking for contributions. This included old friends and people we had worked with. My father showed his support by writing his friends as well. Many sent us money despite our slim chance of success, and we were grateful for every dime we received. Others honestly told us why they could not support us. We were surprised that some ignored our requests altogether. At least, we thought, we had discovered who our real friends were.

Mark created his campaign headquarters—my office—by building a wall to partition off part of our garage. He dragged an old carpet and a few folding tables from the barn at Coosaw to furnish the windowless space. It is an understatement to say that this office was not glamorous! I think we had two phones, and it seemed terribly sophisticated that I could answer the lines from phones upstairs in the house as well.

Mark's sister Sarah was our sole volunteer in charge of signs (often homemade), and she walked any parade Mark and I could not make on our own. We had a few loyal volunteers who came to help lick envelopes or map neighborhood routes for Mark to knock on doors. Mark ordered a whopping two hundred bumper stickers and six large road signs, a meager amount, of course, to cover any congressional district. He treated those bumper stickers as if they were made of gold. He would only let someone have one if Mark was permitted to follow that person to their car to make sure the sticker made it onto the bumper.

Mark traveled the district (still in that stick-shift hatchback), meeting with Republicans, speaking to rotary groups and church groups, and attending fish frys and candidate forums whenever he could. I learned his positions on the issues and spent lots of time writing out answers to the questions each newspaper and interest group sent to us. Mark would then review the answers and tweak them if needed. I would ultimately type out the final responses on Mark's little Apple Macintosh computer and fax or mail them out to the world. In addition to learning of Mark's beliefs in depth, I respected the fact that he wanted to share his thoughts on an issue honestly and earnestly instead of giving the standard political sound-bite answer we were accustomed to hearing. We used this same careful attention when fielding questions on the phone.

On the weekends and many weekdays, Mark set out from our home early in the morning to knock on doors. We decided that he should focus his attention on mostly conservative, Republican districts with people who were more likely to be sympathetic to his message of cutting back government spending and government intrusion in our lives.

Mark wasn't just a deficit hawk on the stump; he also lived that message in the running of the campaign. By February 1994 we had added $19,100 of contributions to our account book yet had spent only $786. Mark's opponents had spent more than $100,000 by that point in the campaign. Though penny-pinching was his nature, Mark seemed to understand that unless we paid attention to every precious dollar, we would easily and quickly be bled dry. There was constant pressure to purchase ads in Republican newsletters or in the local newspaper to keep up with what other candidates were doing. Mark impressed upon me the importance of remaining disciplined, and I followed his lead by managing expenses carefully in the office.

The press pays very little attention to those they think are fringe candidates, and they had lumped Mark in with that crowd. If people think you can't win, many won't show up to volunteer or give you money, even if they warm to your message. This forced us to think more creatively about ways to draw attention. Free press was all we could afford. As he walked door-to-door, Mark started handing out fake billion-dollar bills and told the voters he believed Congress was spending our hard-earned tax dollars as if they were "funny money." This clever stunt brought a bit of welcome and free media attention, but not enough to gain the notice of power players within the Republican Party.

As it happens, even if you are on the same Republican

team, sometimes you are not the right kind of Republican or perhaps you have not paid your dues within the party establishment. This seemed to be the case with Mark—no one within the party thought he had yet earned the right to this competition. He repeatedly drove two hours to speak to a monthly gathering of Republicans in Myrtle Beach, only to be told by the same woman in charge that she couldn't find time to fit him into the agenda. Mark's ideas were part of the Republican Party's stated ideals, and yet somehow the establishment considered him an outsider, not loyal enough to represent the party or its cause.

Mark's message encompassed term limits, too. He didn't want to become a career politician and was wary of those who did. He believed that we should return to the model our country was founded on: a citizen legislature where ordinary people served for a while and then went back to being regular citizens who had to live under the laws they helped to create. He announced he would limit his own tenure, if elected, to just three terms or a total of six years. He also thought that political action committees gave incumbents an unfair advantage, so he refused to take any money from them. If all candidates restricted themselves in these ways, he believed, we'd get more common-sense decisions from our representatives about taxes and the spending of our money. In standing up and offering to limit his own term, Mark set himself apart from the other candidates who may have pledged to support term limits in general, but would not commit to limiting their own.

I think anyone following this congressional race would have been impressed by Mark's integrity, even if they didn't share his political views. I was fully immersed in the day-to-day running of the campaign and of caring for our two young sons (while Marshall had been a very content baby and a good sleeper, Landon had terrible colic and his restless sleep made both Mark and I exhausted in a not very satisfying way!), but even I found time to be impressed. Mark seemed to be hitting his adult stride, and it was an amazing thing to witness.

After spending seven-and-a-half months knocking on doors, driving to every event in the district, handing out fake money, speaking at forums, putting up signs, and handing out bumper stickers, we got hard numbers on how difficult it is to become known without spending money to get out a message. The local paper did a poll of likely voters six weeks before the primary, and Mark Sanford came in fifth out of a field of seven with only two percent support. We found this incredibly disheartening, though not unexpected. I remember asking Mark if all this effort really was futile, but he remained steadfast. Our media campaign was about to begin over July 4 weekend, and that was when we hoped our message could really begin to penetrate.

I continued to draw strength from an increasingly clear sense of Mark's positions on all the issues and also from that elusive thing called loyalty. I had Mark's back, and I got my back up when I found something had been said or written about him that I felt was wrong. If a reporter twisted the truth,

I couldn't sleep until I had set the record straight. In response to an article I found completely misleading, for instance, I sent this rather scathing letter to the editor of the *Post and Courier.* It was printed on July 20, 1994:

No Campaign Deficit

The word "deficit," as defined in the dictionary, means the amount by which a sum of money falls short of the required amount. Deficit spending refers to the practice of spending funds in excess of income, something our federal government does every day. My husband, Mark Sanford, is running for Congress because he is frustrated with the way our government is spending money and the way it is not making common-sense decisions on a variety of fronts. His bumper stickers, signs and stationery all have a "reduce the deficit" logo on them. I was shocked, then, to read an incorrect report in your paper today that Mark had "rung-up" a "deficit" in his campaign.

Mark's campaign has never run a deficit and never will. To date, it has taken in $203,740 and spent $127,885, leaving a cash surplus of $75,854. Maybe your reporter studied accounting at the same school as most of our politicians. Mark has never run for office before, but he decided to run for Congress because he feels so strongly that regular folks, not people closely tied to the political system, need to get involved in government. It is crucial to our future and to that of our children to change the way things are done in our federal government and to start getting decisions from Congress that make sense again.

Mark strongly feels that we all need to stand up for what we believe in. That's why Mark—a "political newcomer," as your paper calls him—has invested money in his own campaign as he would do in any business transaction as well. In addition, he's raised more than $103,000 from individuals who agree with his message of change, more than a dollar for every dollar he's invested himself, hardly "financing most" himself as your paper states. What's wrong with standing up and doing what you believe is right?

Mark believes in campaign finance reform, and instead of just saying he favors legislation that does away with PACs, he has himself refused to take a dime from any political action committee. Mark doesn't just support term limits; he has taken the first step by limiting his own.

Mark is a man of honesty and integrity who doesn't believe in politics as usual or in political rhetoric. I am proud of Mark and of everything he has done in his campaign to date. We need lots of Mark Sanfords in our government and maybe in journalism too.

Jenny Sanford
16 Wentworth Street

As I re-read that letter now, I can remember the visceral feeling, the buzz, that the campaign gave to those close to it. I can also remember well the exciting momentum that started to build once we went on the air with ads. Many seemed to like Mark's fresh face on television, and some recalled reading of his term limits pledge or meeting him when he knocked on their door. When the paper ran another poll on July 31, just over a week before the primary, Mark had jumped to fourth place with fourteen percent in the polls, an incredible jump in a very short time. Mark's candidacy started to really take off, and our garage campaign office finally had a real group of volunteers.

Although Mark began this campaign with his thirty-page paper on debt and Social Security, we learned all too soon how the press can take long, thoughtful answers to questions on issues and reduce them to sound bites, often twisting their meaning, intentionally or otherwise. We also learned that there will always be some reporters against whom we never had a chance: For whatever reason, they were intently against Mark and his candidacy. This phenomenon became abundantly clear when Mark answered a question for the newspaper in Myrtle Beach, one that is distributed in a significant part of the district he sought to represent in Congress. The issue was about roads.

In the historic city of Charleston, there are many who would like to close off the city and keep tourists from entering, the feeling being that if we were to build more interstates heading here we might as well make them one-way as no one will want to leave once they get here. Myrtle Beach could not be more different. They want more roads built to bring more tourists and more revenue.

Mark answered the Myrtle Beach paper's question: If there was a huge federal bill filled with billions of wasteful spending and dozens of bridges to nowhere, but it had a small sliver of money for building roads in Horry County and Myrtle Beach, would he vote for it? Staunchly against unnecessary spending, Mark said he would have to vote against that bill. The reporter printed that Sanford "would vote against roads" in the area, implying Mark was against any road funding.

This created a firestorm so large that we had to spend precious resources defending Mark's position. When Mark personally confronted the reporter about why Mark had been quoted out of context, the writer looked at Mark and replied "life is out of context." It was as though he was as astounded at Mark's and my ire as we were with his journalism. He seemed jaded. Mark and I were much less so back then.

As the primary election drew closer and we started rising in the polls, we experienced the ugly underside of politics more specifically. I had heard of dirty tricks before in our state, but nothing prepared me for just how downright mean the sport of politics could be here. We became the subject of mystery calls to voters, otherwise known as push polls, in which a phony group such as "Citizens on Behalf of Fairness in the Media" calls and asks the innocent voter a question that implies something about a candidate that simply isn't true.

The push poll call is designed to plant damaging associations in a voter's mind that will cause him or her not to vote for the candidate who is the subject of the call. South Carolina is famous for this particular dirty trick. Our state was the place where unknown operatives helped to derail John McCain's 2000 effort to become president by asking unsuspecting voters if they knew McCain had an illegitimate black child. The McCains had adopted an orphan from Sri Lanka, an act of pure generosity of spirit, but the push poll made him sound like a philanderer. For Mark, the implied accusation was a lot milder, but still very damaging to Mark's candidacy if it were true, which it was not. The caller asked: "If you learned that Mark Sanford was a good friend of Bill Clinton . . . would you support him?" (Needless to say, being a friend of Bill Clinton's was not a good thing in a Republican primary.) We also experienced the impact of special interest groups who send out voter guides, sometimes entirely honest and other times crafted in a manner to highlight a specific favorite candidate over others with similar views on the issues.

Looking back now, I see how this was just the first taste of something we would be forced to swallow again and again in each of Mark's campaigns. I look around at the political landscape today and I can still see dirty politics on display at every turn. It was a great place to be in life and in our lives together that we could still be outraged and baffled by these things. I am no less outraged today, but I am no longer at all surprised.

I was personally exhausted as the primary drew to a close, but I have to admit we were also having fun. We had great new friends in our volunteers; we shared enthusiasm and a mission. Doing more with less was part of every aspect of the campaign. Volunteers would color large stickers to attach to our six road signs with short messages that would make them come alive, messages like "Just Three Terms" or "No PAC Money." We also had our small team of volunteers shake signs at the base of the Ravenel Bridge or at busy intersections, all designed to give the illusion of widespread excitement and energy. Whether Mark won or not, we both believed we had run a campaign to be proud of. We shared a sense of purpose and that was exhilarating. For the first time since I had known him, Mark was completely and fully absorbed in something that seemed to satisfy his restlessness, which made me happy to see.

Life as a mom, however, was quite a juggle during this time. Thankfully Landon's colic had passed and he was sleeping full nights, but nonetheless I was stretched thin. I was in the campaign office most of the day while someone watched the boys so I could oversee all activities in the basement office. I would break for lunch with the boys and would somehow squeeze in grocery shopping or time for a well-check at the pediatrician or some other such family necessity.

The boys were now two and almost one years old, and they were able to travel with me to campaign events or to TV stations. They were a draw when we shook hands in the parade at the Hell Hole Swamp Festival or when we went to the

Chicken Bog Fest in Loris. But they were still very small, they needed their sleep, they needed routine, and they needed their parents' attention. Truth to tell, my loyalties were torn as the campaign heated up. I wanted to do a good job with the campaign, but I also wanted to raise my boys well and to love them fully, and there was not enough time in the day to do both. However, my belief that God always seems to put the right people in your life at the right time was soon rewarded. Our house was down the street from the College of Charleston, where my favorite sitter (one who didn't mind Landon's screams) was a student. She moved in with us as the primary neared, which allowed me to work long into the evenings after I'd put the boys to sleep. Having someone I trusted to keep them safe and to be on call for them helped put my mind at ease as we carried on.

As the August 9 primary date approached, I felt as if we were running on adrenaline. Even though I was swept up in the momentum and excitement, I was ready for this endeavor to be behind us. There are many times in life when one feels completely out of balance and this was one of them. I had a purpose then, and it was to fully support Mark's candidacy while balancing the needs of our young family. Fulfilling this purpose was satisfying but doing this well left no time for me, no quiet time for personal growth or reflection or to recharge my batteries. I know I was growing as a person through the testing of our values and through my deepening knowledge of my husband but I couldn't keep this frenetic pace indefinitely. As with so many difficult things in life, I found this time was made easier because I knew there was an end that was clearly in sight.

On primary night, we gathered joyfully with close friends, family, and campaign volunteers at a local cafe. I was dressed in my red-white-and-blue campaigning attire from that day, with Landon on my hip in onesie pajamas and a pacifier in his mouth. Marshall sported Barney pajamas and red tennis shoes. He waved flags and ate cake, all way past his normal bedtime.

We watched the results come in on television, knowing that it would be close. If no candidate earned more than fifty percent, there would be a runoff election in two weeks for the first- and second-place candidates. We expected Van Hipp to come in first, as he was the frontrunner and the political establishment candidate. Our focus was on the pack of candidates vying for second place. We knew we were outspent by more than two to one by two or three of the candidates, yet we believed our disciplined and incredibly focused campaign still stood a hair of a chance. We were quite literally in shock when, with ninety-nine percent of the votes counted, the results were as follows:

Van Hipp	31%
Mark Sanford	19%
Bob Harrell	17%
Mike Rose	17%
Mendel Rivers	12%
Sarah King	3%
John Henry Whitmire	1%

The news reports that night and the following morning described "an electoral Cinderella story" and talked of Mark as a "giant killer," likening him to David from the David and Goliath story. The press was suddenly enchanted with Mark, describing how he "came from nowhere" to win his spot in this runoff. Clearly, they had missed all our hard work! We were exhausted and elated, tired but victorious. And the battle had somehow just begun.

Swept up in a tornado of our own making, we realized that we had to raise more money immediately, film new ads, and work even harder, smarter, and somehow faster to get our message out. Mark was still very much the underdog, but the momentum was on our side. As this was a very conservative district, the odds were good that if he won this runoff election he would be able to win the seat in the general election. Having said that, if he won, we would have yet another exhausting campaign for the election in November. I got tired just thinking of it.

This part of the campaign was different because it was so intense, being squeezed into just two weeks. Van Hipp came out swinging. He described Mark as liberal, a real taboo in a conservative primary. We suspected that Van Hipp was financing more push polls. Implying it was Mark's position on the issue, callers asked voters things such as, "Would you vote for Mark Sanford if you knew he favored legalization of drugs?"

Mark got so riled up by this that he went to Hipp's house in the middle of the night to confront him. When Van opened the door clad only in his boxers, Mark stuck a tape recorder in his face and demanded that he state whether he was behind the calls or not. Van was undaunted by this confrontation. He denied funding the polls, and we couldn't prove that he was doing so. And misinformation-filled mailings to voters continued: literature saying that Mark Sanford was "pro-abortion" and that he was "for universal health care" though neither was true.

Mark and I found these tactics colossally discouraging, and we vowed we would always run our campaign honorably, never saying something through the campaign medium we were not comfortable saying directly to the opponent. We wanted to change the terms of the debate, to actually have a debate of ideas without getting into the politics of personal destruction. At the end of the day, we believed, people liked honorable men and women in government and if we remained loyal to our values, voters would see Mark in this light. At this moment in the campaign, I understood my value to Mark was much higher than just the fact that I was "free." If Mark had spent money to hire a campaign manager, not only would he have used precious resources, but he would likely have been strongly advised to respond to negative attacks in kind, thus compromising those values that I knew were so important to us both.

Unbelievably—to many, even to us—Mark won fifty-two percent of the vote in the runoff primary. What an upset! It seemed to us that the stars were aligning, and the shot in the arm that this win gave both Mark and his campaign staff would be the fuel for most of our future confidence. We celebrated heartily with volunteers and friends and family on election night and my happiness and my pride and my excitement was real. Yet I couldn't wait for the festivities to end so that I could get to sleep. But of course, the activity never stopped. We were immediately swept into the next race for the general election.

This time the Republican Party was united behind Mark. We were one of the hopefuls that would be part of a Republican takeover of the U.S. House of Representatives, and all eyes were focused on winning against our Democratic opponent, Robert Barber. Fundraising was much easier as the national party sent other politicians such as Dick Armey and Jack Kemp down to star at events and help raise more money. People came out of the woodwork to volunteer or to offer their advice or their services. Suddenly the campaign had outgrown the space we had available in our garage, so when a supporter offered to provide us with an office down the street from our house, we moved to more professional environs.

As the campaign expanded rapidly, I tried to step down as campaign manager. The general election felt quite different from our grass roots, ideological efforts at home. More was at stake and the effort was bigger and less personal than when we were working just to get Mark through the primary. I wanted to return to being a mom, but our media consultant pleaded with me not to, as he didn't want us to fix what wasn't broken. Mark understood that I wanted to step back and he understood why, but he begged me to stay on. We had made it this far together, he reasoned, and we had been a winning formula.

I struck a deal of sorts. I agreed to stay, but we would engage others to lighten my load. I know we actually hired one person but there were quite a few people with serious campaign experience who joined us as volunteers, too, and their combined support helped relieve me of the exhausting full-time detail. Nevertheless, we didn't fully trust the agendas of all our new "friends" in this campaign, especially after the day we discovered two volunteers rifling through files they didn't need to be looking through. When they couldn't really explain what they were up to, we asked them to leave. From then on we kept an eye on all unknown newcomers. Mark and I continued to keep the real decision making between ourselves and our media adviser.

Late in September, Mark and I traveled to Washington, DC, so that he could sign Newt Gingrich's famed Contract with America. It was on this trip that we began to feel like we were on a much larger team: We met so many other Republican candidates and U.S. Representatives who all wanted to help us win. As collegial as that began to make us feel, we learned that with these higher stakes came dirtier tricks, and we were naïve enough to take real offense, to be bothered by it. As we arrived at a Republican fundraising dinner that evening, there were picketers outside the entrance. Mark saw a few holding signs with his name on them that said things like "Sanford you're eating the heart of the lowcountry." Mark, honestly wanting to know what he had done that upset these picketers, went up to one to ask him directly. After tapping the man with the sign on the shoulder, he discovered the man had clearly been hired to hold the sign: He had no clue who Mark Sanford was and could barely speak a word of English.

During this brief trip, we also discovered how deeply the opposition would be willing to dig to oppose Mark's candidacy. A reporter we met there showed Mark a full-page ad printed in *Roll Call* magazine and paid for by the Democratic Congressional Campaign Committee that listed ten Republican candidates for Congress, including Mark. On the other column was a list of things these ten had done. The idea of the ad was to match the name of the candidate with their past. The list had all sorts of outlandish credentials like "claims that white, Anglo-Saxon men are an endangered species" or this candidate "claims Greeks and Romans were homosexuals" and so on. I looked at the list and had no clue which act was attributed to the man I was married to. After eliminating the ones I knew could not have been Mark's doing, I narrowed it down to Mark having been a "goose exterminator." I asked him if he'd ever been one. It turned out one summer during college he worked to control the goose population in New Zealand by shooting geese and injecting poison into unhatched eggs, something I'd never known, yet the press had managed to find out before me.

Goose exterminator or not, the contrast between Mark and his Democratic opponent Robert Barber was clear, no more so on display than when Barber falsely claimed Mark opposed hiring more police and that he advocated legalization of prostitution. When asked if he would support a specific bill on crime, Mark responded that he would not because of the wasteful spending in the bill. Barber used Mark's stance, absurdly, to label him as "pro-crime."

When Barber's attacks on Mark's positions on the issues didn't cause him to gain any ground, he went after Mark's personal life. He tried to paint Mark as a wealthy tourist from out-of-state, although in fact the Sanfords had moved to South Carolina from Florida fifteen years earlier and had spent every summer there before that. His tone implied that if you are successful or of means, you are unfit to represent a congressional district. Then he picked on Mark for not voting in every election, as he had not registered to vote during the year and a half he lived in New York City.

In my mind, this just meant he was a normal citizen; when he had moved away he hadn't bothered to change a lot of things, including his driver's license. He had known the move north would be temporary. That "normal guy" image was what we emphasized in our ads. The style was friendly and direct, with Mark speaking to the voters about the issues he cared about, no gimmicks or sleazy attacks. Perhaps that was what made people believe that they knew him. After just a few weeks of running our ads, Mark went from a virtual unknown to someone who was recognized on the street. Suddenly when he knocked on doors, he was greeted warmly. He relished it when someone gave him a thumbs-up or told him they agreed with his positions and would likely vote for him in the upcoming election. I think that even with all the perks and parties and praise that comes with political success, there is nothing quite as empowering in all of politics as the unsolicited thanks of someone on the street.

On election night, almost exactly one year after beginning our stitched-together campaign, we held our celebration at Calder's Pub on King Street in Charleston. Mark won the election with sixty-seven percent of the vote, almost 95,000 votes: a very healthy total. We had run an almost flawless campaign—rising from two percent in the polls in just four months. We won despite spending much less money than our opponents in each of the three elections. By focusing exclusively on the issues Mark cared about, we ran an honorable and effective campaign, never once taking our eye off the ball. Republicans were elected in many districts all across the nation that same night as control of the House was transferred from the Democrats to the Republicans for the first time in decades. Through our victory we were joining up with a movement that pledged to take the country in a bold, new direction.

For me, however, that election victory was not as exciting as the primary had been. In such a heavily Republican and conservative district, Mark's chances had been very good once he became the party candidate. My excitement was at the prospect of getting back to a more normal life. Marshall was now speaking in full sentences and potty training while Landon had just taken his first steps. They were swept up in the activity too but I yearned for more time with them, time when we could enjoy being instead of doing.

In an interview I gave to our local paper the next day about the election and my expectations, I said boldly that I'd never liked politics, didn't want to be involved in politics, and, "now that this campaign is over, I'm finished with politics." The story went on:

> "I was exhausted," she said. "I couldn't answer one more stupid question. I couldn't smile at one more person. I missed being with my children."
>
> Mrs. Sanford isn't sure what comes next—whether she'll stay in her Wentworth Street house or move to Washington.
>
> Right now, she says, she's focused on something more immediate. After the ten houseguests leave and the pillows are put away, she's going to spend a night at home with her family. No one else. She'll wear blue jeans and eat popcorn. She won't answer the phone. Better yet, the phone won't even ring.
>
> After that, she wants to see her friends, read something beside political treatises, and play some tennis or golf. (*Post and Courier*, November 10, 1994)

Little did I know then that the busyness was far from over, the houseguests would linger, and my desire for time alone with my family would become the fight of my life thereafter.

Looking back I now realize this was the beginning of Mark's unyielding loyalty to the conservative principles of fiscal stewardship and limited government. It is this unyielding loyalty to principle that is so rare in politics and yet it is perhaps this same unyielding focus on these conservative principles that caused Mark to lose sight, over time, of his personal values that I think matter more. It is one thing to campaign on the issues but I was soon to learn that in elected office one's adherence to the issues is challenged continually. Mark's loyalty to the issues from then on would be seriously tested and so would his loyalty to me and to himself.

SIX

At the moment when Mark won his seat in Congress, we were the closest we'd ever been, victorious in something that we started from just a table in a chilly garage. My commitment to manage his campaign was one of those here and now choices. Mark had a dream and working with him to achieve it was a way to help him feel more fully alive. When I said I'd do it, I was taking the long view, imagining we would reminisce some day about what great fun we had that crazy time he decided to run for Congress. I gave it my all, and improbably, I became the wife of a politician.

We made another quick series of decisions about what seemed to make sense in the day to day. A congressional salary is nothing compared to Wall Street standards, or of one in real estate, so we had to think carefully about how we were going to live within our means. The first decision was whether our family would move with Mark to DC or remain in Charleston.

The House of Representatives' two-year term makes it the elected body most responsive to the people. What this meant for a political newcomer like Mark is that he had to be home in the district as often as he could on weekends to remind the voters who he was and what he was doing for them. The government will cover the cost for a congressman to travel home if his time home includes official business. The government will not, however, cover the cost of flights to DC for visits by the representative's spouse and children. We decided we would see more of Mark if we remained in South Carolina and saw him on trips home. Logical, yes, but amazing to me now, how naïve I was to agree to being a single mother four or more days a week. In my own defense, I know now that raising the boys didn't give me much time to think!

Shortly after he was elected, I traveled to DC with Mark for orientation and to help him look at apartments. Of course, he was only looking at cheap places in neighborhoods that seemed very dangerous to me. When he decided to sleep in his office on a futon, my mother called me, alarmed.

"You can't let him sleep in his office!" she said.

"Why not?" I responded. As if I could somehow get Mark to change his mind!

"Well that's just not okay for anyone to live that way, and what will he do when you visit?"

"Mom, I think it's just fine." I said. "I saw the awful apartments he wanted to rent and I would be worried for his safety in them, and mine as well. If I were to visit him there, I would likely find myself cleaning the place. If he sleeps in his office, when I visit once or twice a year, I can stay in a hotel for a nice break and he can visit me," I explained.

She saw immediately where I was coming from and agreed we had a good plan.

When I think back to the two of us at that time in our lives, I marvel at how wonderfully naïve and idealistic we were. We saw the world as black or white and were dismissive of those who saw it in shades of gray. Through the campaign for Congress, my love for my husband deepened as I saw him refuse to be swayed from his beliefs in order to pick up a few votes or an endorsement. He would rather lose the campaign than win it through sleazy compromises, and my idealistic young heart swelled with pride to be married to such a principled man.

But after our principled campaign, we took a crash course in the reality of rules-to-live-by for elected officials. It became immediately apparent to me that campaigns never end; they are a constant part of public life, and public officials follow an entirely different set of standards. I didn't believe that Mark would get caught in these traps because of his loyalty to his core beliefs.

We've all seen many times how a candidate promises to lead courageously and follow ideals, then the endless horse trading of being an elected official causes those ideals to slip. In the crude reality that exists behind the scenes, every issue has a history, constituencies on differing sides, as well as lobbyists for or against flattering the legislators and offering them trips and lavish meals to curry favor. In order to get anything done, representatives trade a vote on a bill they don't really believe in for promises of support on another bill. Bit by bit, those initial ideals and goals get chipped away. All the more reason, Mark and I believed, to keep them in focus and make every decision guided by a conscious appreciation of them. Mark's constant struggle to hew to his own standards of frugality, for instance, was not just a virtue he would promote in government, but one that he would demonstrate in his daily life in Congress.

From the very first day, he closely watched expenses in the office, requiring the staff to save paperclips and copy on the reverse side of used paper. As long as the federal budget remained unbalanced, Mark refused to take a pay increase, instead donating the raise the representatives voted themselves to charity. (In his first year in office, with what he saved on administrative costs, Mark also returned more than $200,000 in funds to the U.S. Treasury.) Plus, on principle, he refused the franking privileges, which allow representatives to send mail for free. Mark believed this amounted to a campaign subsidy that protected incumbents at the expense of citizen legislators like himself.

Once he got to Congress, Mark's Cinderella story captivated the national media, which was charmed too by the fact that Mark wasn't just a deficit hawk on the stump. He caught the first possible plane home when voting ended, bringing his dirty laundry back each weekend. He bragged about how he could survive two weeks on a $20 bill by grazing at lobbyist-funded receptions and being driven by staff to required events. When the press found out where he was living, images of the futon in the middle of his grand congressional office space made great television. Mark found the attention difficult to refuse. In truth, he relished every bit of the glare and soon grew to seek it.

As the media lavished attention on him, the people in our district became more aware of his budding national presence. They called or wrote to tell Mark how proud they were of his election, and how hopeful they were that he would succeed. Where fundraising had been nearly impossible during our first campaign, suddenly unsolicited checks filled the mailbox, along with offers from complete strangers who wanted to host fundraisers for Mark's reelection.

I learned immediately of "the almighty schedule" and of the importance of fighting for open time for our family. The scheduler booked Mark's time in five-minute increments throughout each day and into the evening. If Mark allowed it (and he largely did), he could fully book each evening and weekend with speeches, dinners, parades, or even with travel to spots around the world to learn more about the issues being debated and discussed in Congress. There were many weekends when Mark was home in name only. He'd show up, hand me his laundry, spend a few precious hours with the boys and me, then be off to an all-day marathon of public events and fundraisers.

In the meantime, I was just as busy with our little constituents, to whom I was connected in a way that no one but they and I could see or appreciate. Mark's connection was necessarily diffuse and to a broad public. Mine was intimate. I was wholly and completely engaged as I held down the fort in Charleston with my pack of babies, another of which, Bolton, arrived in the second year of Mark's first term. One night in particular reminds me of the very different kinds of lives my husband and I were leading.

When Marshall was three and a half and Landon was two and a half, both had a violent stomach bug, and I found myself running around cleaning up after each one, repeatedly changing sheets and pajamas while trying to comfort them both and nursing baby Bolton as well. At one point, I got Landon back down in his crib and had Marshall with me in my bathroom. I pleaded with Marshall to wear a pull-up diaper because I just couldn't keep up with all the mess. He insisted he was a big boy and didn't need a diaper anymore. During a moment of clarity, I realized I would not win a negotiation with a stubborn toddler, so I got Marshall a pillow and blanket and placed them in the tub, and said, "Well then son, you are just going to have to sleep in the tub!" At the prospect of sleeping uncomfortably and alone in the bathroom, Marshall gave in and agreed to wear the diaper "just for one night." Whatever you might say about the maturity of his colleagues, these were not the kinds of negotiations Mark was having in Congress!

The boys and I had our own pleasures and routines. I treasured my time with them. We loved sitting together with take-out pizza and watching movies while just a few channels away their dad cast his vote on an important bill on C-SPAN. Mark had a rare opportunity to serve the country, and all of us were pitching in. I reminded myself that my lot was no different than the wife of a busy salesman and a lot better than the spouse of a solider serving in one of our wars. And at least I could see my husband on C-SPAN if I really wanted to tune in. Job asked: "Shall we indeed accept good from God and not accept adversity?" We had been richly blessed. Doing my small part to accommodate Mark's busy life while focusing on the blessings underfoot was minimal on the adversity scale; it was not too much to ask.

Knowing Mark's extremely frugal habits, I knew not to expect much from Mark for birthdays or for Christmas, even if I felt it was surely nice to be remembered every now and again. After our first big primary and run-off wins in 1994, Mark surprised me over a romantic dinner one evening with a beautiful gold pin, a laughing elephant I have worn plenty over the years he has served as a Republican. Once in office, however, his habits deteriorated and he even forgot my birthday once. Thereafter, I nudged the scheduler to remind him. (My birthday is on September 11, and since 2001 Mark has learned to remember it without a reminder.)

One birthday during the later congressional years, Mark decided to do something very nice for me. He had a friend pick out a diamond necklace and he had a staff member hide it in my closet. Then he faxed clues to the campaign office in our basement as to where I should look to find my birthday gift. I had the boys join me in the scavenger hunt and, working together, we found it. I loved it! Not only did I love the necklace, but this reminded me of what I loved about Mark Sanford. The scavenger hunt was clever and his notes and clues were ever so boyishly sweet.

A few days later, he arrived home from DC. We had dinner guests, and I was proudly wearing my lovely new necklace. As soon as he saw me wearing it, he said "*That* is what I spent all that money on?! I hope you kept the box!"

He returned the necklace the next day, thinking it was not worth the money he had spent. He could see I was disappointed, but he promised to make it up to me. In truth, once I knew he thought he had overspent, I also knew it would pain him to see me wear the necklace had I insisted on keeping it. I wouldn't have felt comfortable wearing it in his presence, so what was the point? I had married him, after all, knowing he was not a big-spending Wall Street type. I remained thankful for the thought and the sweet scavenger hunt nonetheless.

I wasn't the only one to bear the brunt of Mark's frugality. Mark had a standing weekly movie night with fellow congressmen Lindsey Graham and Steve Largent and they would rotate who was responsible for the movie tickets and snacks. When it was Mark's turn to get the popcorn and soda, Mark chose the best deal. He bought one large bag of popcorn and a jumbo-sized Coke with three straws. I'm not sure if Lindsey and Steve thought Mark's decision was stingy or hilarious. But his explanation was simple and true to form: The Coke had free refills.

In all fairness, I realize that seriously caring about saving money is an admirable (and rare) quality in a politician. Mark's frugality isn't for show. It is in his core. Spending money gets his attention. I learned to use this to my advantage.

We arrived home late one Sunday evening in January 1997 from a congressional retreat in Hershey, Pennsylvania, with Marshall and Landon. We'd left baby Bolton at home with a sitter, Zetta Brown. Upon return, Zetta told us Bolton was sleeping soundly upstairs, but she thought she had heard a bird in the house.

When I went upstairs to unpack and get ready for bed, I discovered two bats sleeping peacefully in my sink. I called for Mark, who calmly got the bats snug in a t-shirt. The older boys were enthralled as he gently released the bats out the front door. We proceeded to unpack and tucked Marshall and Landon into their beds. Then I went to bed too, only to find bats swooping through my bedroom as soon as I turned out the lights.

This time I called frantically for Mark, and he got a tennis racket and started whacking at bats throughout the house as the boys slept. (I later learned it is against the law to kill bats, a federal law Mark called worthless once I informed him of it.) Nine bats later, we went to bed, though I lay awake and kept one eye open for bats for too long.

Though Mark thought doing so was a waste of money, the next morning, I called a pest control man named John to make sure the bats were gone. John discovered that a cap on the chimney had been torn back, allowing space for the bats to enter the house through the fireplace. He did what he felt was needed and told me once the bats left to feed that evening, they would not be able to return. But at dusk, the bats were swooping through the kitchen, and I was a nervous wreck! Bats in the house seem to swoop right at your face, making you want to dive for the floor. Mark killed a few more that evening and then chuckled at my fright as he departed for DC the next morning.

I couldn't take another night of them. I vacated the house before dusk and took the boys to sleep at a friend's down the street, while giving the keys to the house to my new friend John.

It turns out bats can hibernate inside. We needed to be patient a bit longer as he enticed them all to leave. Not a job for me. I felt I was wearing out my welcome with the three little boys at my friend's house and also felt little empathy from Mark, safe in his batless office in DC.

So, on Thursday I moved with the three boys to a suite in a local hotel and called Mark to tell him that I was not moving back in until he had slept in the house for at least two nights without seeing a bat. Facing the prospect of paying for an extended hotel stay, Mark sprang into action, effectively dealing with every last bat. We happily returned to live together as a family Sunday night.

Mark described his time in Congress as similar to being a member of a fraternity, bantering about ideas with colleagues and remaining friendly despite disagreements. He also enjoyed standing on principle to nudge change in one direction or to keep change from happening too fast in another direction. As engaged and happy as he seemed, I began to wonder if remaining true to what he believed was making him a very lonely or unsatisfied man.

As a staunch fiscal conservative, Mark was on the fringe of his party in Congress. He was one of a handful who opposed the relaxing of our nation's mortgage rules in the 90s, for example, when few could conceive of being against a law that claimed it would encourage home ownership for everyone. He made many lonely votes against large military bills too, because of the tendency to bloat military spending with unnecessary earmarks. His principles required him to oppose things—opposition that later would be used to portray him as heartless. He was one of the sole votes against a breast-cancer stamp because it cost money and he thought it was merely feel-good legislation that would ultimately lead to more government creep. In some cases, it was he and just one or two others voting together on an issue.

At one point in the middle of his second term, we rented a house on the South Carolina coast for a much-needed vacation and the differences in our pace and lack of connection caught up to us. I was feeling the strain of living apart, and I was also exhausted by my time alone juggling the demands of the boys. On a walk together alone along the shore, I tried to explain my frustration. I didn't begrudge Mark his time away from the doctor's appointments, the school events, and later the homework, because I saw Mark's career as a family effort. But his work protected him from the ordinary, day-in, day-out connection with the boys, I explained, and as a result I felt he was becoming out of touch with us. My job was tapping into the most tender parts of my heart and soul. His job demanded that he be calculating and sometimes manipulative. I was growing more vulnerable, and he was forming a hardened shell.

For his part, Mark complained that I didn't understand the stress and pressure he was under. We didn't say it in so many words, but it was clear that while both of us were rarely alone, in our own distinct ways, we were lonely.

What we did say led to tears—mine—and to a soul search about whether we should even stay married. I know many marriages weather similar discussions, sometimes with one spouse threatening to leave. Neither Mark nor I threatened to leave, but we were both working hard to be understood and falling short. Our geographic distance was yielding a real emotional distance as well. I questioned then whether he really understood me. I assume he questioned that about me as well. His seeming inability to understand my needs and my worries also made me question if he truly loved me. I don't know if he could say the same, but in many ways I think we were discovering things about our marriage that made us each afraid for the future of it.

At the same time, this heart-to-heart served as a wake-up call of sorts. We were acknowledging that life had become hard, but we still loved each other and also had a family that we both dearly wanted to hold together. We both hoped that life would get easier, that we would enter into a new and more manageable "season" once his time in Congress was through. In the meantime, we agreed that his career was an important part of both of us, and that we didn't want to upend it by continuing to move apart. Divorce just wasn't an option. We wanted to stay together and we would. Besides, I believed him when he said he would end his service in Congress after six years. At the moment of this painful argument, we were about halfway through.

SEVEN

EVEN WITH A RENEWED AND EXPLICIT COMMITMENT AFTER OUR argument on the beach, Mark and I spent less and less time together during his last term in Congress. By then our home was on Sullivan's Island. We had sold our house in Charleston and bought an informal and seemingly indestructible cinder-block one near the beach on Sullivan's, an island at the mouth of the Charleston harbor. I had instantly fallen in love with life on Sullivan's. The pace, the proximity to the sea, and the simplicity of the home itself suited me and gave me great happiness, even with Mark gone so much. This still-cherished year-round beach retreat has given us all some needed space—indoors and out—though Mark has taken refuge in its walls less than the rest of us. Indeed, at that point he was returning home infrequently on the weekends, traveling more often, expanding his knowledge of the issues in South America, Khazakstan, Bosnia, India, you name it. I got used to having him gone and justified it by his need for adventure and travel and, yet again, reminding myself of that finish line that I could see coming toward me in the distance. This was a fairly lonely existence for me all the same. Mark was seeing the world, but I wanted him to see that this world that he and I created was just as interesting. I worried that so much of it was slipping away from him unnoticed, never to be reclaimed. That restlessness and drive I had admired so much when we were courting was causing him to look outside the home for adventure, while I believed the adventure of my life was nestled in my arms.

I now have some perspective on how this snuck up on us. Our entry into this unreal world started quickly and, at first, we were both caught up in the excitement of it all. As soon as we won that first campaign for Congress, the phones were ringing with other politicians congratulating Mark on his win and suggesting one course of action or another. The press wanted interviews and sound bites for the evening news. Congressional tabloids asked for photos and bios to profile the newest members of this exclusive club. Lobbyists called to flatter Mark as they pitched their causes and successful businessmen wanted to meet him for lunch or dinner to ensure their interests were protected. The accumulation of this special treatment was no doubt a big part of what disconnected Mark and me from each other and what disconnected Mark from the values and priorities he once held dear. On

Wall Street, I saw many a man whose ego grew as his income rose and he got more attention from those around him, but nothing I saw there compares to the immediate and transformational ego-stroking of politics.

I can see now that it was naïve to think that marriage and family would take the edge off Mark's frenetic hunger. After all, right at the moment when I had achieved a lifelong goal—the birth of our first son Marshall—Mark said he was bored. He wanted to be stretched to the limit, and as much as he loved me and our growing family, domestic life didn't do that for him. Motherhood was stretching me physically and emotionally in ways he couldn't share and that he didn't appreciate.

Many marriages suffer when the partners start to prioritize differently and then grow apart from one another. The more I saw Mark pack his schedule, the more I tried to become the antidote; I worked to balance the frenzy. I supported his campaigning and entertained with him as much as possible when he was home on weekends, but I also would regroup and slow down during the week when he was away. When he pulled us into his freneticism, I pulled the other way, trying to carve out time for us to recharge instead of deplete our batteries.

This push-pull was probably futile. I grew to see I couldn't fix him and he didn't want me to slow him down. I couldn't find his happiness, but I could make the effort to connect with my own.

Though I admired the way Mark persevered in the aftermath of his father's death, over time I less charitably saw the mirror trait of that perseverance: stubbornness. He did things his way, and his way only, on a host of fronts. Still, I knew the stresses Mark was under and the challenges he faced so I had to pick my battles with him carefully. We had our shared goals, our family, and our focus on his career to bind us together. My feeling was that anything that distracted from those things was something I could let go of since there were so many pressing responsibilities that needed our full attention. As a modus operandi, this more or less worked because our basic values remained shared.

Call it perseverance or stubbornness, Mark didn't make it easy for himself to succeed in Congress. He would regularly return from DC frustrated that he had "nothing to show" for his valiant efforts; at least, he said, I had the babies to show for my hard work. His popularity was sky high with the voters in our district because he took a stand against wasteful government spending. This made him a maverick among his peers. Fighting so many majority-supported big bills made it hard to champion laws of his own; he wouldn't support other representatives' bills so they had little motivation to support his. Opposing legislation often did succeed in keeping federal spending lower than it would have been but it wasn't like a notch on the belt of success to be remembered for. He also wanted to enact laws he believed in, including some that would further restrict rampant government growth, and on that front, he frequently faced defeat.

I tried to help Mark see that success—as he was coming to define it in his day-to-day work—didn't correlate to self-worth. Through the highs and lows of his own life, my father has demonstrated that success is a personal thing defined by the way you live your life every day, and by what you do with the skills you have and the blessings you have bestowed on you. I praised Mark for his hard work. I praised him for the hard work of opposition. My praise was never quite enough. Like many men, his personal bar for success is satisfied by more tangible things. On the weekends at home when not campaigning, I would often find Mark on a track hoe at Coosaw from dawn till dusk creating a pond or even digging a giant pit for the boys to play in (and, possibly, risk their lives!), complete with a PVC pipe for chicken fights and a zip line. He explained he loved seeing his progress "one scoop at a time" and knew at the end of the day just what he had succeeded in creating. In this—building something—he could feel satisfied.

One brilliant fall Sunday at Coosaw, we took the boys deep into the woods for a picnic. I spread a blanket under the bright blue skies in a large clearing, while Mark got the boys to help him start a fire in a grand stack of logs left by a crew that had been logging timber there. Shortly after the fire was lit, the wind began to pick up. After finishing our simple lunch, I had to pack away the blanket and leftovers as the breeze strengthened. In no time whatsoever, the flames were two stories tall and the wind was blowing some of the flames in the direction of the neighboring stand of pines. I was terrified watching our little boys trying to beat back the flames with skimpy branches. Alarmed, I drove with the baby to a local store to ask the old men gathered there to help while the storekeeper called the fire tower. Eventually a small plane dropping water from above helped get everything under control. As we left for Charleston and the airport so that Mark could catch his flight to DC, a passing fireman asked him if he was related to Congressman Mark Sanford. Neither denying nor confirming his identity, Mark just smiled and moved along.

This was the first time I witnessed Mark communicate something less than the truth, an episode that I have considered and reconsidered in different lights over time. Had knowledge of this gotten out, who knows what the media would have done with it?

The longer we stayed in politics, the more contemptuous I became of this media circus and its carnival atmosphere complete with barkers and stunts and people who are trying to trick you. This battle over who controls the image affects everything the politician and his family do. It felt to me as if they were always looking for the slightest mistake or for something they could twist and sensationalize. As a result, we all found ourselves calculating how whatever we did might look to an unsympathetic audience, even if we had done nothing wrong.

Mark had made a mistake building a fire in those conditions, but it's the kind of mistake that happens all the time and the wind had shifted and strengthened. Would political pundits weigh in, using it as a metaphor for Mark's judgment? Perhaps a future opponent would use the story to blame Mark for taking advantage of the same state resources whose budgets he cut back. In that way, it is understandable that he wanted to keep this quiet. On the other hand, his fear that the story might show him in a poor light caused him to sacrifice a piece of his own integrity. The same Latin words that mean "not" and "touch" are behind the word integrity. A person of integrity is whole, complete, untouched. People of integrity are the same in the dark as in the light. The fear of how this would look caused him to withhold the truth then, and in time he would do so to the press, and to me, again.

One of Mark's trips during his last term in office was to India, something that incited a mundane crisis, but one that made me wonder again about our future together. We were flying to Seattle over Memorial Day weekend for my brother's wedding. Mark thought this would be a good time to pick up some extra income and a way to put into practice something he'd learned watching so many poor in India: Don't be so attached to things. From his distant perch in DC, he rented our house to some Citadel grads. He didn't consult with me about this, and then he got the dates wrong, renting it two days before the boys and I were supposed to leave. I was suddenly, frantically, cleaning the house so that it would be presentable to the renters, then we had to move somewhere for two days (an expense in and of itself—the net gain on this weekend was not much!) so that I could attend Landon's kindergarten graduation before we flew west.

Mark flew directly from DC to Seattle, so I flew with all four boys (all under the age of eight at the time) and met up with Mark there. On the long flight, Blake (one and a half) conveniently got sick and I was more than happy to pass him to Mark's clean arms upon arrival. My nerves were frazzled from the trip and I was fuming.

Our relationship was chilly that weekend, to say the least. Once alone, I told him I thought he was incredibly self-absorbed and disconnected from reality and from me. I reminded him that the special privilege of marriage is that the two partners get to know each other in a deeper way than the rest of the world, in fact, one hopes, almost better than they know themselves. I thought the world that Mark lived in illuminated the image, the superficial, a part of him that was calculated to be unknowable. It wasn't the first time I thought it, but it might have been the first time I articulated it: The more he succeeded politically, the more time he spent living in that persona, and none of it served our marriage well.

Mark knew he was still in the dog house even after we returned from the wedding. He sought help by calling the leaders of a fellowship he and several other political figures attended when in Congress and asking them to speak with me. I wasn't pleased to do so. I figured that Mark had portrayed me as an irrationally angry wife and that they would gang up on me to convince me to drop this issue. They did anything but. All three of the men comforted me by telling me that I was right to be angry with Mark. But a member of the group, whom I'll call Jack, advised me that staying angry with Mark was not an option. If I wanted to heal the relationship, I had to open my heart and be kind, even if Mark was in the wrong. *They* would work on Mark. We even went so far as to talk about sex, and he told me not to withhold it as punishment as that would make everything worse. The marriage and family mattered more than this one issue, he advised. I was buoyed up by this support and all the new things I had to consider when looking at Mark and the pressures he was under, the strange way public figures live their lives and are with their families. My meeting with these men from the fellowship was the first time I heard an explicit description of the term "disconnect" in reference to politicians, and it seemed apt. I think one even called it "the Congressional Disconnect." Move on and let go of the anger I did.

I had become pregnant with baby number four just as Mark's final campaign for Congress began. Mark was so popular in his district that he had no major party opponent so our campaign was fun, consisting mainly of public appearances in front of friendly crowds. But Congress doesn't stop for childbirth. I was scheduled to have my labor induced so that Mark could arrange to be present for the birth. Right up until that day, however, we worked. Two days before we were scheduled to be at the hospital, Mark and I spent hours on the tarmac at the military base in Charleston shaking hands with folks at the air show as our boys climbed in and out of military helicopters, planes, and tanks. It was hot and humid, and I gripped my hands tightly beneath my giant belly, fearful the baby I was carrying might drop flat on the steaming airstrip if I let go.

Mark's friend Senator John McCain, who was quietly beginning his run for president, visited our home the next day, a Sunday. Mark had a group of about thirty men for lunch to meet him. I served sub sandwiches from the deli on paper plates, about all I could handle at that stage in my pregnancy. Mark prompted McCain to tell stories from his time as a POW and gathered our boys to listen. The hubbub of boisterous political talk died down as the whole group leaned in to hear his tales from the Hanoi Hilton.

One story that particularly moved Mark and me was about McCain's cellmate, Mike Christian. Every day, no matter what horrors he and the other prisoners had endured, they rose to pledge allegiance to the flag. Mike Christian had sewn a replica of the flag onto his shirt for the soldiers to look at when they pledged. When the guards discovered it, they ripped the flag off his shirt and beat him severely. Upon return to his cell, he quietly began sewing on another flag. He was, quite literally, willing to die for his flag and his country.

Mark and I drove to the hospital the next morning and Blake arrived easily, another healthy baby. Mark and I decided to give him the middle name of Christian, in honor of the patriot-soldier in McCain's story. From the first, Blake seemed calm and steady, something that still serves him well as the youngest of this brood. Mark then caught the midmorning flight to DC in time to vote in Congress. Having these kids was so easy for Mark, I think he would have been happy with ten sons, but the pregnancy and birthing of them all was clearly less easy on me, and we had decided that these four healthy blessings were just enough. The next day I was scheduled to get my tubes tied.

As I was wheeled in for surgery, the nurse asked me why I didn't have anyone with me for support. I was surprised at her question. It hadn't really occurred to me that I would need Mark there for the surgery. What would have been his role? He could wring his hands and worry about my progress from Washington just as well as he might have from the waiting room. In any event, I told her my husband had been with me the day before, but he'd gone back to work. Maybe her question was perfunctory, or maybe she truly was surprised to find me alone. Either way, I can see now that our circumstances were unusual. Somehow, I had become perfectly accustomed to managing alone. My independence gave Mark tacit permission to leave that day, and, I can't help but wondering, later as well.

Late in the 1990s, Mark was nearing his last term in Congress and his anxiety about what would come next in his life was active on all fronts. Impressed by the dedication and professionalism of the military he saw through his activities on the Hill, he began to regret that he had never served. He lamented the increasing disconnect between the rights that go with being an American and the responsibilities of citizenship. So, during his last term in Congress, he enlisted in the Air Force Reserves. In addition to seeing this as a responsibility of citizenship to participate, he also wanted to set a good example for our boys. By the time the military accepted Mark, he was already running for governor, but he decided to honor his commitment, and I was proud of him for that decision, even as I understood that he would now have even fewer weekends at home for the family.

Perhaps part of Mark's anxiousness was also because he was approaching forty, and he wasn't taking it very well. By that point, ten years into our marriage, I was accustomed to his restlessness and list making, but the confluence of passing that age marker and ending his time in an important job made this transition more fraught than others had been.

Mark's zest for living life to the fullest comes, I think, from his fear of dying, and of dying young in particular. I think this feeling overcame him as a young man when he quite literally put his father in the ground. He often spoke about how short life is and how he needed to fill every minute. Mark is not alone in his point of view, of course, but the worry that stuck most in my mind was his sad feeling that past the age of forty he would have "no more good summers." As someone who treasures every day, every season, this statement was and is unimaginable to me. On the brevity of life, we both agree. The difference is how we chose to spend our time. I wanted to savor each moment while the boys were young and he clearly wanted not a moment to sit still.

As a result, the small signs that he was starting the inevitable process of slowing down unnerved him. When his back hurt or his sore knees kept him from running ten miles at the same pace he had when he was younger, he took this as evidence of his approaching death. He brushed aside my suggestions that he adjust his exercise pattern to suit his age. He was going to fight this at every turn, never giving in to the inevitable.

He's not alone in this fruitless struggle. Our culture celebrates the hardness and vigor of youth, the edge that comes with it, and seemingly has no time for its opposite. But I believe in what Marcus Aurelius said: "There is change in all things. You yourself are subject to continual change and some decay, and this is common to the entire universe." I feel strongly that the best way to age is not to fight it and the change that comes with it. Rather, I try to embrace it and grow through it.

Whatever our differences though, his concerns were genuine and, I have to admit, the inspiration for a great fortieth birthday party.

Naturally, I threw him a surprise party. He thought he was going to give a formal speech at Middleton Plantation but on his way to the building in which he expected to speak, his friends and family emerged from the gardens all dressed in funeral wear. Everyone wore black, the women were handed lace veils, and someone even came dressed as the grim reaper. The special feature of this celebration wasn't presents. Nearly everyone there had written a eulogy for Mark. His worst nightmare—that he would die at forty—

became the inspiration for a memorable celebration that, I hoped, showed him how much he was loved.

Mark was a good sport about the party, though perhaps the rest of us thought it was a lot funnier than he did. In trying to gently—or not so gently as the case may have been—rib him about his worry, I hoped to relieve him of it. I wanted to show him that life was not anywhere near over and that he was not now on the path to decline. I wanted him to see that there was much fun to be had then and ahead.

EIGHT

I EXPECTED THAT IN 2000, WHEN MARK KEPT HIS CAMPAIGN PROMise not to run for a fourth congressional term, he would return to a smaller-scale life with me and the boys. I believed Mark would be ready to return to working in real estate and be even more successful for all the knowledge he gained in Congress and all the powerful and important contacts he had made while serving there. All of this, combined with more time with me and the boys, would give him, I hoped, many more ways to quantify his accomplishments, to feel successful and finally appreciate that his life had meaning.

We never really had the time to find out. It wasn't very long before people from across our state started to urge Mark to consider a run for governor, probably one of the hardest jobs in politics. As with his first run at Congress, Mark's appetite for a challenge was whet at the prospect of seeking a job where it would be difficult to get elected. He would yet again have to win a tough primary against six other Republicans and after that, he would face a well-funded Democratic incumbent, Jim Hodges. He was also energized by the idea that if elected, it would also be a challenge for him to succeed.

South Carolina state government operates under a truly archaic system. After the Civil War, politicians worried that a heavily black constituency would some day elect a black man as governor. With that in mind, then-governor Ben Tillman led the effort to change the state constitution dramatically, stripping the governor of most of his powers. The legislature, a variety of constitutional officeholders, and various unelected boards and commissions have largely run the state ever since. The governor is often the first to be blamed when he can't fulfill his promises, even though the mechanism of state government is arranged in a way to block him at almost every turn.

Mark spoke with advisers and consultants and friends about whether or not to run. The more people he talked to, the more excited he became about the possibility of making real change. Instead of accepting the idea that he would be working within a highly restricted environment, he wanted to run on a pledge to reform the government and to bring fiscal responsibility, common sense, and a businesslike approach to all the affairs of our state. He saw the need for a governor to look out for the interests of the state as a whole, as a chief executive should. Just as important to him was preserving the

Our wedding day,
November 4, 1989

Past bedtime, primary night, 2002

Campaigning was always a family affair.

Boyhood fun at Coosaw, the Sanford family farm

Blake meets President George W. Bush.

Mark's swearing-in for his second term as a U.S. Congressman, January 1997

Fun at the Governor's Mansion

More fun with friends, celebrating my fortieth birthday at the Mansion

The boys with my father, Christmas 1999.

Sisters Kathy and Gier with me and Mom

Gubernatorial inaugural ceremonies, January 2007

Mark's third and final term as a U.S. congressman, summer 1999

Our maturing family, May 2009

aesthetic look and feel of the state. He had strong feelings about protecting open space, keeping rivers pristine, and saving forests. He wanted to avoid the kind of overdevelopment seen in South Florida. This was and still is a rather rare stance for a Republican. With these as his issues, we calculated that there was a slim chance he would win.

Mark also consulted the boys and me about his decision, and we all were unified in our support. The way I saw it was not so dissimilar to when Mark decided to run for Congress. The prospect of running for the state's highest political office energized Mark; the intense focus and his ideas for new possibilities for the state clearly would make him happy. I also figured that this would be a fifteen-month undertaking from the day he decided until what might well be a primary defeat. If Mark happened to win, I would at the very least look forward to all of us living together under the same roof, unlike his time in Congress.

He wanted to go for it; I pledged my support. But this time, I was adamant that I would not serve as campaign manager.

Mark hired a young woman to handle his schedule and another to manage incoming money and plan fundraisers. Next he hired a press secretary who, though worth his weight in gold, came cheap (which Mark liked) because his most recent job had been playing in a rock band. Many others showed up to volunteer through that first summer and the momentum started to build, but Mark was frustrated having to manage the staff and seemed unable to find a manager to his liking. As the summer wore on, he began his push to get me to change my mind and return again as campaign manager.

Although I was proud of running his successful congressional campaigns, I knew from experience the toll the job would take on the boys. I also knew it would likely unhealthily shape the kind of time I would have with Mark. These were reasons enough to refuse the role, but there was another big reason I worried about. If I took the job, ours would be the only statewide campaign in South Carolina ever led by a woman, much less a wife. There were—and still are—many in the political and power base in the state who sneered openly at me and suggested it was not my place to do this work. I have come to love South Carolina deeply, but I'm not blind to the challenges still in place for women there. There still exists an old-fashioned chauvinism that would have women stay out of positions of power or strength. Perhaps they forget that South Carolina has plenty of strong and successful women in its history.

One such famous trailblazer (and a personal hero) was Eliza Lucas, who, in 1738, was left in charge—at the age of sixteen—of her family's three plantations in the lowcountry. In addition to overseeing the plantations, she educated her younger sister and some of the slave children, pursued her own courses in French and English, and did legal work for poor neighbors. All the while she experimented with a new crop called indigo. By the age of nineteen, Eliza Lucas became the first in South Carolina to successfully produce blue dye from indigo, ultimately leading to great wealth for the area. After marrying Charles Pinckney, Eliza had four children, including two who were key players in the move toward our nation's independence and the war that followed. Not only did Eliza Pinckney accomplish great things when facing life's challenges, she also *gave back* to the world. She was a loyal wife, she raised successful children, and she left an indelible mark in more ways than one.

Mark knew that these were my standards of personal success and he worked on me—sometimes playfully, sometimes seriously—to see that in coming back on as campaign manager I would have the opportunity to meet them. He continued to plead his case, and six and a half months into his campaign I gave in, plain and simple. As fall began and the older boys returned to a school routine, I secured help for the little ones and started to pitch in formally with the campaign.

Win or lose, I knew that for me, the standard of success in this campaign wouldn't be measured by the simple metric of whether Mark won. As the boys were older, their needs were more complex. I felt my efforts would be a success if I ran a well-organized, ethical campaign while never feeling that I had neglected my children.

Toward this end, I tried to stay close to home. The ground floor of our Sullivan's Island home has a concrete slab floor and exposed heating/AC ducts. Until Mark announced his candidacy for governor, we used it as the boys' playroom, a place where they could do whatever they wanted, and we also had one room there that served as Mark's office. Thereafter, we rearranged the entire space for the campaign office, bringing down folding tables as desks and adding computers and phones as needed. By closing off a corner near the bathroom, we created a bedroom for campaign workers, bringing two sets of bunk beds from the barn at Coosaw, and putting the boys' old dinosaur sheets on them. It became known as Jurassic Park. We also used the old garage area and divided that space into more campaign offices.

The average age of the group downstairs was about twenty-two, which gave me, at age thirty-nine, the right to refer to my "little kids" upstairs and my "big kids" downstairs. Before long it was anybody's guess as to what or who I would find when I went down the steps. I felt sometimes as if I were in charge of a large group of animals at a zoo.

When the boys returned from school—Marshall in fourth grade and Landon in second were in school until three o'clock and Bolton and Blake were home all afternoon—they added an entirely new flavor to the campaign. At any given moment, we'd have big and little kids jumping or wrestling together on the trampoline or shooting hoops in the driveway. The boys made a game out of catching the press secretary on breaks outside for a smoke. We had a bunny, Sully, who came downstairs with Bolton to visit often. Our kids charged through the offices dressed in armor with swords, or they might swap football cards with one of the campaign workers, or ride bikes to get snacks together down the street. We had a cat then named Spot who did not take kindly to the new routine at the house. He randomly threw up on the computer keyboards and sometimes would disgust us further by presenting a creature caught on his hunt.

Things downstairs were active into the evening most nights. I would cook dinner upstairs and soon was cooking for extras, happy to have others so dedicated to our new mission. I did my best to juggle it all and usually enjoyed all the activity in the house. There were certainly times, though, that I wanted to close my eyes and wish it all away. I reminded myself again and again that this pace and this activity would not, could not, last forever.

A campaign is an intense affair and a statewide race has so many overlapping facets that it becomes a big boiling pot that needs to be kept bubbling without spilling over. While we all had a great deal of fun in the campaign, and some of the daily volunteers or employees are now lifelong friends, it would be a lie to say that I never lost my cool. I understood that loose talk, loose finances, or shaky attention to detail can all unravel a campaign. There was a place at the bottom of the stairs where we hung beach hats and baseball caps. I would bring a worker to this spot if I needed to have a stern or serious discussion about an issue in a semiprivate location. Not surprisingly, the gang began to speak of getting in trouble as being "taken to the hats."

Fundraising in politics is also a 24/7 job—not something I ever enjoyed, but it seems a necessary evil throughout the political process. We raised and spent more than $7 million in small increments through mail or events in South Carolina and beyond during that campaign. We had stacks of shoeboxes filled with checks around the office and systematically made sure that every donor received a letter signed and personalized by Mark.

I tend to think of the ability to raise money as an indication of the strength of one's ideas and of one's ability to communicate those ideas. Mark was good at it; I was not. I chose to abstain. On most evenings Mark was off raising money, while I focused on keeping things going at home. As we got closer to the election, I attended fundraisers if they were large ones or appeared with Mark when needed, but I held off as long as possible so I could stay at home with the boys. I know Mark gave back to the country and to the state through his service as a congressman, governor, and in the Air Force Reserves, work of which we can all be proud. Yet I wonder what it cost him to continually be at functions with his hand out asking for money. I have long believed that it "is in giving that we receive" and that generosity helps keep a person focused on important things in life outside of the self. The constant take, take, take is one of those things that serves as another way to isolate a politician. In this way, the easier it got for him to ask others for money, the more he moved away from our youthful idea of a citizen legislator and toward the identity of a career politician.

Even though fundraisers weren't my thing, the boys and I did need to be on the road with Mark for appearances. While I care about being generally well-groomed, on the campaign trail in a high-profile race the idea of "appearances" gets ratcheted up several notches. I always needed to be aware of how I looked or how our children looked or acted in public. The public pays close attention to adorable little boys, but unfortunately, little boys are hard to control, especially when one or more of them is potty training. I had always encouraged the boys to simply go outside discreetly if they couldn't hold it. This saved many a pair of pants during potty training. But in the early stages of the campaign, Blake, then aged two, dropped his short pants to relieve himself unceremoniously on a gravestone in an old churchyard as we were leaving a crowded church service. I had all the boys dressed in matching outfits, so I couldn't pretend this boy wasn't my own—tempting as that might have been at the time—so when a woman there called Blake to my attention, I grabbed him up and hurried to the bathroom hoping not to make a scene.

On another occasion, I had all the boys on stage in Columbia as we awaited the arrival of President Bush, coming in to campaign for the party. I had given them clear expectations for their behavior: They could run around onstage until I told them it was time to stop and then they were expected to sit very quietly through the president's speech. One of the secret service men was getting anxious about Blake, who was dancing on the stage in his cowboy boots waving an American flag in one hand and his blankie in the other. I didn't see much harm in Blake entertaining the crowd as they waited in the heat, and I promised him the boys would behave when told. On cue, when President Bush arrived they quieted down and sat patiently through the speech. The next morning, however, there was a photo in the paper with the president at the podium and just behind him to the side was Bolton (maybe five) with his head in his hands looking incredibly bored! Mark was disappointed in me for not coaching the boys to look interested, but I myself was proud of their good behavior. There's only so much you can ask of a child, and sitting quietly through a political speech was the limit!

One time we traveled from city to city campaigning over a weekend, ending up at a fundraising event. After the event we loaded the boys in the car and headed to a friend's house in the country near a town called Estill. We arrived past midnight and moved the boys to beds while they were asleep, something that had become a common occurrence on the campaign trail. We were staying in a private cabin and in the morning awoke in a room full of large stuffed game on the walls. When we asked if the boys knew what city we were in, one responded "Africa!" Sometimes I, too, felt like we were lost on safari.

In the weeks leading up to the primary the boys, out of school for the summer, joined us on a tour of the state in a Winnebago we dubbed the Caravan for Change but that they referred to as the Win-a-Bagel. We did our best to make things fun for the boys—they played GameBoys, tic-tac-toe, or cards, watched movies, and ate fast food. It was pretty clear that they often had a blast with all the campaign volunteers along the way. Certainly that is my hope. Surely they missed out on fun with friends during that time, but it was a family adventure all the same.

The boys did journal on occasion during the campaign so

I do have a way to test my impression against their own experiences. Marshall's journal says, "We went in the caravan and it was huge! We went around the state to different places shaking signs and screaming vote for Mark Sanford. . . . It was crazy but it was worth it for dad." Landon felt a little differently: "I went in a win a bagel and a van. It was very boring. It felt like we were in there for a month." And later: "My mom is mostly on the computer and has lots of calls. My dad has a lot of calls to." He was right about that. We were nothing if not busy and constantly on the phone but I hope that they will have a generally—if not specifically—positive memory of their political experience in time.

When we won the primary and the campaign for governor moved to an office outside the house (in addition to needing more space, it was hurricane season and our beach house was thought to be vulnerable), I more or less moved with it. I had a great young girl who helped to care for the boys during this crunch time, and I trusted that they were okay, but I missed them terribly. I missed seeing them every day after school, and I hated not knowing what they were doing for homework or eating for dinner on the many nights I wasn't home to join them.

But I was also very proud of them then, and I remain so now. I know they were as tired of the campaign as we were and yet I asked them to persevere for just a few more months and to do their best in school in the meantime. They did beautifully. It's amazing what kids can do when you have faith in them.

As soon as Mark won the Republican nomination, he became the immediate enemy of the incumbent governor and the existing political establishment. I learned to live with the knowledge that a good portion of the state disliked Mark because of his party affiliation and that they disliked me by extension. If nothing else, the campaign process and then life in the public eye taught me that you can't really live to make others happy. You also simply can't correct all the misperceptions about you or your spouse or your intentions on any given event or statement. Mark understood before me that it is much easier to let things go, than to try to right every wrong. This is, in fact, one of the best things Mark has taught me: to let God be responsible for righting any wrongs.

By the time Mark ran for governor, I had learned this lesson well. When I think back to how incensed I could become when Mark was misrepresented in the newspaper or by his opponents, I marvel at the energy I put into fighting back, writing that impassioned letter to the editor, for instance, to correct the record on what I now see as merely a slight. I suppose the world of politics had toughened my skin, but with four children to be responsible for during Mark's run at governor, I had less time and energy to fight back than when I had had only two. In addition, people now knew what Mark stood for and what he had tried to accomplish when he was in Congress. We didn't have to work so hard to create a good identity for him and craft his positive message. Much of that work was already done.

And then there's the simple truth that I had come to understand and that I wanted to model for our kids: What matters most is how you live your life, not what you have to show for it. I ask myself if I have tried my best to love my family, to improve my character, to make a positive impact on the world in some small way. I know who I love and I know who loves me, and if I have made a positive impression on others, that's great. But if someone out there doesn't like me or Mark because of something they read in the paper or heard on TV, then that is okay with me too. I had come to understand by then and live by it still today: At the end of the day I need to be happy with myself and my own behavior in light of the person I know I can be and in light of the person I want to be in the eyes of our Lord, the ultimate judge, the only one that matters.

Although the pace was hectic and I went to bed exhausted nearly every day, I didn't pray for relief from the challenges in my life. I was fully committed to this new quest, and I wanted to meet the challenges that came my way. Instead my prayers were for discernment in setting priorities, protection for us and our boys, and strength to proceed. Then, and during other trying times of my life, I found meaning in an old Jewish proverb: "I ask not for a lighter burden, but for broader shoulders."

Incredibly, we won the election. At the celebration at a local restaurant there was more media than I had ever seen and homemade signs in the crowd saying things like "Thanks for running an honorable campaign!" We were thrilled and exhausted and Blake fell asleep in my arms as the night wore on. As it was a school night, I wanted to get the boys home. I tried to cut out early, carrying Blake and leading the other boys through the kitchen instead of working my way through the crowds. A policeman with a gun and wide-brimmed hat came up to me and said "I'll take him Mrs. Sanford. The car is right outside." Policeman or not, I wasn't about to pass my sleeping child over to a stranger with a gun, and so I thanked him quickly and told him I had my own car and was happy to take the kids home myself. Then it occurred to me to ask "Do you even know where we live?" "Yes ma'am," he replied. "We've been watching you there for two weeks."

That was my first clue about how significantly our life was about to change. Once again, we had achieved success at the polls by focusing on the campaign tasks at hand and juggling our family, hoping to make a difference. We had not spent one minute thinking of or planning for the future in the event we were to win.

We looked upon Mark's new job as quite an honor and a time to truly serve and to make a positive difference for our boys and the future of our state. We were tired but enthusiastic, exhausted and yet energized, hopeful and yet realistic, and encouraged too because this time, we would all be living in the same house, sharing the journey together. I was about to find out all that would come with this "free" house and the full price we would ultimately come to pay.

NINE

INAUGURATION DAY WAS COLD AND CRISP WITH A BRIGHT BLUE SKY, picture perfect and a bit surreal. As I helped our sons, then ages ten, nine, six and four, get dressed for the formal inaugural ceremony, I thought about how these four little boys would be walking out of the house and into state history.

Yet there I was doing the ordinary things that every mother does: making sure their clothes looked just right, that they had enough socks and underwear in their overnight bags to last until our things arrived from Charleston in a week, and checking that their book bags held what they needed for school. The ordinary and the extraordinary collided when we opened the front door and the security detail whisked us into the state SUVs to begin our first day as the First Family of South Carolina.

The Sullivan family motto, learned from my grandmother Nana when we were children, was A.Y.T.C.—adapt yourself to circumstances. My aunt Gier, my dad's sister, a mother of nine, lived just a few houses away when I was growing up. She was the reigning authority on adapting to whatever was thrown her way. I took up the mantle for a new generation when my family moved into the governor's mansion. From the day of the election forward, all circumstances were new: finding a new school, moving, and learning how to oversee the mansion.

A few weeks after Mark was elected, the curator led me on a tour of the mansion, one of three historic homes on nine acres in a secluded complex. We walked past an emerald green lawn and blooming camellias as the curator described the gardens in summer, bountiful with incredible roses, irises, daffodils, and hydrangea. Built in 1855 to house officers from a nearby military academy, the state turned it into the governor's mansion after the Civil War, when much of Columbia was destroyed by fire.

Mark and I thought of the mansion as the people's house, and we took our responsibilities as custodians seriously. As we walked inside I saw how the house was in great shape after the previous administration had spent millions on renovations. The curator ushered me into the grand, gleaming marble Hall of Governors, past somber portraits of Mark's predecessors. Everywhere she pointed out exquisite museum-quality antiques, some upholstered in vibrant silks and pristine cottons, many that had been donated by prominent families. As we walked the hallways, I noted the fragile light fixtures, historic paintings, and exquisite battleship silver with growing alarm. We were moving four bulls into this china shop!

The day of the inauguration, the security team seemed as nervous about meeting our brood as our boys were excited about discovering where they hid their guns. They drove us directly to Mark's new office at the Capitol and then escorted us as we walked behind the procession of the cross, mace, and legislators to the inaugural prayer service while bagpipes played. For the first time, I truly felt "handled" and I was quite thankful. After the chaos of crisscrossing the state with four boys during the campaign, I could relax and enjoy every moment. Then we made our way through the waiting crowds, past dozens of cameras and blinding flashes, and back to the Capitol where Mark was sworn in.

I was awed. So many people had put their faith in Mark, and we wanted to live up to their expectations. Being First Lady and living in the governor's mansion was an honor, something to be lived fully and absorbed wholly. I knew I would struggle to keep in focus the fact that I was Jenny, a wife and mother, long before I was First Lady of South Carolina. Throughout Inauguration Day, the boys constantly offered reminders of where my focus should be.

After Mark was sworn in, we hosted a luncheon for all the constitutional officeholders at the Lace House, adjacent to the mansion. Then we held the traditional governor's open house. We stood in the Hall of Governors, greeting people who had waited in the cold for hours to meet Mark and me, warmed by hot cider and cookies provided by the mansion staff. I remember Bolton, then age six, running in from the other side of the hall screaming with glee, "Dad, this place is *incwedible* and you ought to see the kitchen!? They have bwownies, Little Debbie cakes, evewything, and its all FWEE!"

Together he and his brothers already had covered every inch of this grand house, while Mark and I had yet to get above the main floor. As we stood shaking hundreds of hands, the boys were running all over the mansion, finding secret staircases and alternate routes between the floors that allowed them to avoid the formal rooms and the waiting public. When they tired of that, they snuck their friends past security to join them on the lawn.

There were moments when I just wanted to dash off and find out what they were up to, but I couldn't budge. I was so delighted when I heard a familiar voice yell out, "Oh my goodness! What is the fastest-talking girl in the Midwest doing married to the governor of South Carolina and living in a house like this?" It was Julie Joyce Kenary from Winnetka, the friend with whom I lurched around Wisconsin back roads on a summer afternoon trying to master the stick shift. She'd traveled all the way from Boston to surprise me! Comforted to have someone there who "knew me when," I too felt I needed to pinch myself to make sure this was really happening.

After that and the inaugural barbecue, I could hardly stand any longer. We'd smiled until our cheeks hurt. When

Mark and I finally went upstairs to get ready for bed, we were exhausted, yet filled with pride and great hope in our grand new home. I was pleased I had worked with the staff to give the mansion some personal touches for our first night there. I'd sent ahead family photos and favorite paintings of the low-country, which they hung around the family quarters and the public rooms. We'd also sent a bunk bed to add to the beds already in the mansion. Marshall wanted his own room, and there were plenty of bedrooms in the mansion, but Mark believed in carrying on as he and his brothers had, and I agreed that sharing a room was yet another way they might learn adaptability.

We tucked them into their beds and made our way, weary but joyful, into our new bedroom. Our family was beginning another exciting journey through unknown territory. I myself stumbled looking for light switches during the night. The learning curve would be steep.

As First Lady Iris Campbell told me, living in the mansion was "like living above the shop" and she was so right. Our rooms were at the top of the long staircase in the entrance hall and they were not fully closed off. We could hear the events and tours below, and they likely could hear us too. When guests often exclaimed, "This house is beautiful! Don't you just love living here?" I would smile and politely respond, "It is a beautiful home and there *is* so much that comes with this house!" Yes, and even more than I expected on that first day as First Lady.

In the first week, I discovered that the boys required a new set of rules. I found myself yelling, "Boys, don't throw those balls! You might break the chandelier!"

Marshall's pragmatic response: "Whoever heard of a chandelier in a playroom?"

Balls, swords, and toy guns had to remain outside or in the pool house. Running in the house or sliding down the banister was discouraged, rather ineffectively. At first, I said no scooters in the house. I relented when the boys showed me how well the wheels glided on the marble floors and in the kitchen without leaving any scuff marks. We had great wheelbarrow races in the marble hallway and even whirled each other around in the wheelchair we kept for elderly or disabled guests. Thankfully no one went through the glass doors.

The boys also played manhunt or hide and seek with the aid of the mansion's security cameras. I'd hear one of them at the bank of security monitors yelling to another outside, "He's under the big oak tree!" Once, the boys were playing hide and seek with friends inside the mansion, and security called me in to look at one boy who was hiding in the industrial dryer in the basement. The guard was worried for his safety. I chuckled at this clever hiding spot. I was only worried about the dryer.

I realized quickly that each time the boys had friends over, I needed to line up the newcomers outside the front door and explain the rules before entering, including, you break it, you pay for it. Our only mishap was a science experiment with fire and wax conducted in the dining room. Needless to say, the boys soon found out how much it cost to refinish a table.

When we had been in the governor's mansion just a few months, Blake decided to take the elevator to go upstairs for bed. The elevator got stuck, and he was trapped inside for forty-five minutes, a long time for a small child. The security team called me down to watch Blake on the elevator camera recording his every move. First we turned the power on and off, trying to reboot the system. That didn't work. Next we called the elevator company, but the representative who had the right key was three hours away. I went to the elevator door to keep Blake comforted while the staff tried to solve this problem. Finally we had to take the option everyone wanted to avoid: a 911 call to the fire department, which also had a key.

As soon as the firefighters left, a reporter called asking why fire trucks had been at the governor's mansion. On the front page of the paper the next day was a photo of Blake under the headline "4-Year-Old Survives Elevator Scare." Ever adapting, we used the experience as a lesson to the boys that actions have consequences. They should think, we explained, before getting ideas about pouring suds into the mansion's fountain or pulling a false fire alarm, anything that might alert emergency authorities and thus the press. Learning to be on guard for the press has thus far helped keep the boys from embarrassment, but all the same, I regret the loss of innocence and boyishness that accompanies the grown-up-too-soon requirement to be ever conscious of one's public image.

In these unique surroundings and with this schedule, I constantly struggled to give the boys normal responsibilities, such as regular chores. I didn't want them getting used to living a life of luxury. I asked that they make their beds daily, feed the dogs, and clear the table. But even that last simple request had to be modified for mansion living. I would have liked them to clear the dishes to the industrial kitchen and rinse and stack them at the sink. One sink, however, featured a hose with a nozzle that hung from the ceiling, a tempting weapon if there ever was one. After several epic water fights, I asked them only to clear the plates and dishes from the table, no rinsing required.

In addition to managing the boys, managing the mansion took more time than I had expected. The mansion was broke. Most of the funds appropriated for that fiscal year were gone, and we still had six months to go. I had to somehow find the money to continue the events that "the First Lady *always* hosts" and more. I worked to make sure that we didn't have to close the mansion, as Mark had suggested to the press. I'm a believer in leaving things better than you found them, and I certainly didn't want to allow this grand old complex to deteriorate on my watch. I raised money privately to help finish out the year and set out immediately to cut costs and reorganize the staff.

First, I eliminated the high-paid position of mansion director, and I took over those duties myself for free, learning on the go. Then the new chef discovered that the outgoing administration had burned most of the kitchen files, including financial records, event details, recipes, grocery information, and items to guide us on how to keep the mansion running. Suddenly I was managing a large staff with well-defined, though limited, duties without a guidebook. Some people just washed dishes while others only helped in the kitchen. After the first week, a staff member told me about a new crisis. We needed to hire an additional person to help the woman whose sole duty was keeping up with the cleaning, as she needed help with the ironing.

"The ironing?" I asked, amazed. "Please tell me what, exactly, requires so much ironing?"

She had been taught that the First Family must always look pressed and perfect, and thus she routinely ironed every shirt, all shorts and pants, even underwear. The sheets were washed and ironed every week. Now that there was laundry for six people in the First Family, the ironing responsibilities would surely be too much for just one person who also was charged with doing the cleaning.

"You've got to be kidding me!" I laughed. She obviously had no clue about Mark Sanford, a guy who prided himself on saving money on dry cleaning by making a starched white shirt last ten days. The notion of taxpayers funding someone to iron his underwear was absurd!

I chuckled as I led the woman to the dryer and showed her how we Sanfords "iron" polo shirts, shorts, pants, and underwear: we removed them from a dryer while hot and shook out the wrinkles before folding and placing the clothes in a drawer. Changing the linen every two weeks was sufficient for me, and my kids wouldn't notice, I assured her, if they were ironed. I told her not to bother. Crisis solved.

After that, I instituted a team approach with adaptability as the new mode for everyone. I asked the staff to have an open mind and to think on their feet. Someone doing laundry might be expected to serve when the governor entertained guests and someone helping the chef would also be expected to load the dishwasher when needed, and so on. It was not long before the chef and I figured out who worked well in this type of setup and scaled down the staff accordingly. This reorganization saved the taxpayers more than $1.5 million over the years and has allowed us to operate without further private funds.

In addition to reorganizing operations at the mansion itself, I knew we had to attack the long-term problem of maintenance on the historic property. There was a nonprofit Governor's Mansion Foundation, and I decided to raise money to modestly renovate the empty Lace House so it could be rented for events and generate income for the complex. Mark's mother is a concert pianist who had studied at Juilliard, and she performed beautifully there to help us raise funds. When the renovation was complete, the Lace House soon became one of the top places in Columbia to host a wedding. The house ultimately netted hundreds of thousands of dollars in profits, which is in turn used for upkeep on the property.

The boys and I also wrote a children's history book called *Mischief in the Mansion* to raise money for the Foundation. I'd been giving the boys a daily business lesson on the way to school. Driven there in a state vehicle, I'd read them highlights from the *Wall Street Journal* and quiz them on how the news affected stocks. "The price of oil is way up today boys. What does that mean?" Mark had opened each of them an account with five hundred dollars so they could trade. They began watching the market carefully. As a result, they didn't like the fact that they didn't profit from the sale of the books, but we learned about producing a book and marketing it all the same. By combining the small profit from the book, fees from the rentals, and Foundation funds, we then renovated the historic gardens. This further increased rentals there and improved access and use by the public.

Living a life with so many formal ceremonies offered us other great parenting opportunities. We could teach the kids how to be polite young men who knew how to conduct themselves with our company. If we had formal dinners or receptions, we would encourage the boys to join us in welcoming visitors. We chose carefully which dinners we wanted them to attend, only requiring them to be there when we hoped they might learn something from the guest. When the dinner was just for adults, we asked them to come downstairs to shake hands around the formal dining table and then return to do their homework upstairs. If the English cut-crystal chandelier shook, we knew a game of tag was taking precedence over their studies. This was wonderful boy noise to me. I didn't want to sanitize their home experience too much. Yes, they were greeting formal guests who sat around a table under a majestic chandelier, but sometimes they were barefoot and sometimes in mismatched pajamas. However they were dressed, they made me smile and helped keep my perspective grounded.

The boys weren't the only ones learning about protocol and etiquette. We entertained Madame Wu Yi, a vice premier and at the time the highest-ranking woman in China. The staff and I studied the rules of Chinese decorum and how they acknowledge a respected visitor, rules that were very different than the way honored guests are entertained in the west. The guest of honor had to sit facing a certain direction, we used red and yellow flowers arranged in numbers favorable to the Chinese, and we avoided anything white so as not to offend. Guests had to be arranged for a predinner meeting specifically according to rank, and we had to figure out the pecking order exactly. Mark was away on military duty for that event, and thus I adapted and was intent on making a good showing all on my own. I was proud that we made no mistakes.

With Mark as governor, things for us as a family changed in some ways for the better and in some not quite so. Living again under the same roof, Mark was often there to put the boys to bed and out of that grew his cherished routine of telling them a Bible story or lesson for the day. Yet we were still at the mercy of the almighty schedule. Mark was back into the life of five-minute meetings and thirty-second sound bites. For his schedulers, the public came first. This was a constant battle, and it was easy to get worn down. There were many nights when he was out giving speeches, being the featured speaker at fundraisers, or traveling the country and the globe for state business. Even nights at home were often booked for receptions and other official events. Still we had more family time than we had had when he was in Congress. On the nights when Mark was home, he attended many of the boys' sports events, and he truly delighted in riding bikes with them or playing sports on the lawn. We grew to savor the occasional evening we had when it was just the boys and us.

There were extraordinary occasions for the boys too. Once we had an event at the mansion where there were NASCAR cars in the driveway and Tony Stewart landed on the lawn in a helicopter. (Blake conveniently had a cold and had skipped school that day.) They loved it when Steve Spurrier, coach of the Carolina Gamecocks, would come by or Dave Odom, the basketball coach. The boys became avid fans of the USC teams and so I tried to get used to the notion that four sons wearing hats that said "COCKS" was something of which a mother should be proud.

When we returned from a ten-day trip in August 2003, we discovered the mansion had developed a different kind of life of its own: black mold that was growing up the walls in the hall outside our bedroom and on every item of clothing and every pair of shoes in our closet. This was despite the fact that the air conditioner had been running the entire time we were gone. The arm of the bureaucracy that governed expenses at the house—the Budget and Control Board (BCB)—said that all we had was a tiny humidity problem and that everything in the house was fine. If it was *my* house, I said, and I had just spent all that money renovating it, I would get everyone who had had anything to do with the air system in to figure out why this happened.

Alas, it was not my house and clearly, governor or not, we were not in charge. The BCB worked to reduce the humidity but ignored the possible cause of the mold—government housing and bureaucracy at its best. Mark wouldn't let me pay someone to look into the problem, so I asked an engineer to volunteer his time. He concluded that there was, indeed, a problem in the house. No surprise to me. Still the BCB stonewalled me until I literally had to threaten in June 2004 to sue a bureaucrat over our own health and safety. The threat worked and soon efforts began to fix the problem. We decided the safest course was for us to all move into the one-room pool house. Getting permission to sleep in the pool house took some doing too as we needed approval from a number of state and federal agencies to do so, but it was surely safer than breathing the toxic mold.

Despite the six of us being crammed into that one room for weeks on end, I have a fondness for that pool house. One of my cherished memories of our time at the mansion took place there, and it has nothing to do with mold and is unrelated to swimming in the pool.

Near the end of Mark's first term, Bobby McNair, the son of former governor Robert McNair, asked if he could have a reunion of sorts in the mansion with other sons—most now grown men—of South Carolina governors.

Bobby arrived with five other sons of governors on a weekday evening when it was pouring buckets of rain. Mark was away for military service again, but the boys and I showed the group around the house so that they could take a look around their old home once more. We ended up relaxing in the pool house where everyone told stories of the hijinks from their time there.

Jim Edwards told of an inmate who chased another with a knife from the kitchen before disappearing on Jim's bicycle, never to be seen again. During our tenure, inmates from the Department of Corrections worked almost exclusively outside on the grounds, but in earlier years the house was staffed inside and out with inmates, often then referred to as trustees. We heard about inmates picking locks on the refrigerator for a governor who was hungry and of inmates actually teaching some of these boys how to shoot guns. Imagine that!

One man remembered when there were goats on the property and others told of getting drunk in the pool house or with the security detail when they were teenagers living there. One told of a faux pas he made in front of the press, cameras rolling, when he mistakenly ate the fancy pat of butter, thinking it was a mint. They all recalled sliding wildly down the banister and attending parades and festivals all over the state. Michael Hollings recounted his mother's request that a trustee bring in his new baby brother to show to the dinner guests at the formal dining table. When the trustee arrived, he presented baby brother Fritz to the guests on a silver platter.

Like veterans of the same battles, the men and boys at the gathering also compared notes on their time spent in the shadow of a father who was governor.

Bobby McNair had called for this reunion, and it was becoming clear why he had done so. Bobby was in a serious battle with cancer, and perhaps also in the process of evaluating his life. At the end of the evening, he looked at our young boys and summed things up. "I want each one of you to know that there has not been a day in my life when I didn't walk down the aisle of a church or the aisle of a crowded auditorium when I didn't feel the eyes of those in the room looking at me while they whispered, 'There goes the son of the governor.' Well I want you to know that while you will always be the son of Governor Sanford, much more importantly, each one of you are who you are all on your own first. Each of you is special and unique and has survived life in this place and you will go on to live lives of your own independent of your dad or who he has been and what he has done. Yes you'll always be the son of a governor but you will always be *you* first."

In light of Mark's recent actions, I can appreciate what a gift Bobby's perspective was to me and an even more important gift for our boys. The challenge for any child is to develop a true sense of who he is. The child who develops a solid sense of self-worth independent of his parents, his siblings, or his circumstances is best equipped to face the world. Many of us try to live up to the expectations of those who precede us, which shades our sense of independence or worth. I can only imagine how difficult it is to be raised as the son of a successful governor, and then as a son of a man known for something less reputable altogether. I hope as the boys go forward they can remember Bobby's caution to be themselves first.

TEN

In the summer of 2004, the black mold in the governor's mansion drove the boys and me to the beach house the minute school was over. Mark stayed in Columbia during the week, sleeping in the pool house while the workmen attacked the mansion. He joined us at the beach on weekends. After the hothouse of the capital, the summer was blissfully uncomplicated. We spent our days by the water with my girlfriends and their families. As the children played, we read books, we barbecued, we gossiped, we relaxed. For the first time in a while, I could breathe fresh air. Best of all Mark and I were in a pretty good place. Though we were both incredibly busy, we'd been living under the same roof at last, and with that proximity, I'd fallen in love with Mark all over again.

One sign of our reconnection was that when I had a hysterectomy that August, Mark was at my side for one long, sleepless night in the hospital. After I was discharged, he took the boys back to Columbia, giving me ten days by myself at the beach to rest up before accompanying him to New York for the Republican National Convention.

I luxuriated in this time alone. The surgery had rendered me pretty immobile, but every day I walked to the beach at least once. I read lots of books and reflected on where I was in life. I felt myself aging, and the changes in my mind and body felt good. I yearned to soften into a slower kind of life, something more tender, and with less conflict. My childbearing years were definitively over, but instead of feeling that as a loss, I was filled with hopefulness about what was to come for me and Mark in time. However long he would remain governor, I knew there would be an end to the busy political life ahead. I found myself thinking again about Galatians 5:22, the same scripture Mark had listed as a spiritual goal when we discussed them nearly fifteen years earlier in New York: "The fruit of the Spirit is love, joy, peace, patience, kindness, goodness, faithfulness, gentleness and self-control." We had, in fact, lived that Galatians verse, except for peace. I could see that peace on the horizon. Peace would come to us when Mark stepped out of the limelight.

By that summer, we had lived together as a family for almost four years, but it wasn't until we moved into the mansion that Mark truly came into his own as a father. There I could rely on him to help me discipline the children, which was a huge relief after the congressional years. Gradually he started taking over their spiritual guidance too. As governor, he had an "Open Door After Four" one day a month when any South Carolinian could speak directly to him. People of all backgrounds came seeking assistance. Their stories were often heartbreaking to hear, and Mark was a spellbinding storyteller as he retold them. The boys listened over dinner, drinking in his stories from those afternoons. Often Mark would end on a lesson from a Bible verse, and they'd discuss it for a while or continue with the lesson as he tucked them into bed. Mark seemed to enjoy this too. He expanded his repertoire to tell stories from politics, or from his day at the Capitol. These sessions filled a great hunger the boys had for more time with their dad.

During this time Mark took it upon himself to create what he called the Sanford Family Constitution. When he read it to us over dinner one evening, I nodded in agreement. Everything in it described my own belief system as well. I was impressed that Mark had found time to create the statement, but I shouldn't really have been: The process of quantifying his beliefs and goals was reminiscent of the goal itemization he'd introduced to me all those years before. This document described a vision for our family in which "God is glorified and the communities each of our lives touches are better because of the lives we live. Toward that end, our mission is to be a nurturing, loving and fun safe harbor and home place—where each member is loved unconditionally for who they are, where values are instilled, and where each person is encouraged to develop their talents, find their passion and pursue it with excellence to indeed glorify God and make the world a better place." The family constitution also talked about the things we value: love, faith, passion and excellence, hard work, appreciation, honor and integrity, fun and stewardship and responsibility.

I have a difficult time now looking at this family doctrine in light of Mark's recent actions. That summer, though, I wanted to think of the good times we had and the better times that were to come. The demands on all of our time were significant, but we were settling into a routine as a family and enjoying respite and time together as best we could. I was learning how to seriously prioritize my time, and once again, I focused on the fact that the busy life wouldn't last forever. I was even feeling content.

George Orwell says, "To see what is in front of one's nose needs a constant struggle." In relaxing into my optimistic vision for the future, I now see that I wasn't acknowledging how disconnected Mark was becoming from his stated Sanford Family values.

A governor necessarily has to have a team of people to schedule his every move. If Mark agreed to attend a meeting or to make a speech, he had someone at his elbow jotting down that commitment. At the end of each day, he'd receive a schedule for the next one so detailed it would even advise him what to wear. He no longer had to think about how to get places. His security detail drove him. People everywhere wanted to have their picture taken with him or just shake his hand. I, too, had staff to help coordinate my days, but I wasn't surrounded by "yes" folks, ready to jump to attend to every need.

During the campaign, Mark had promised a lot to his constituents, a very ambitious agenda, and many voters admired his willingness to take it all on. He didn't just want to govern the state, he wanted to reform it, cutting spending and growing the economy instead of the government. This rookie governor, a stranger to the ways of the Capitol, picked a fight with the old boy network, asking them to abolish entire programs and dramatically cut services or merge longstanding agencies.

Mark railed against the legislators who campaigned as deficit-conscious conservatives but stuffed the budget with questionable projects for their districts. As part of his campaign to reform the way government does business, he challenged the legislators to repay a state deficit (the existence of which was unconstitutional) before adding new programs. They paid some off but proposed new spending before finishing the job. That spring, Mark captured the public eye and the national spotlight by carrying two squealing piglets he named Pork and Barrel to the floor of the legislature. The legislators hated how this made them look, and they blustered about lack of decorum in the hall of the legislature. But it worked. They adopted Mark's policies, fully repaying the debt. I was proud of him, but he wasn't making any friends; in pushing so hard for his fiscal principles, he was attacking many within his own party.

With so much underway, Mark was never off duty. He

was besieged from many sides during his day job and simultaneously raising money already for reelection. I was frankly amazed by how he survived. I had experienced the pressures of Wall Street, but they were nothing like what a governor faces. He was elected to serve *all* the people, not just the shareholders, or the company bottom line. Plus he had determined enemies within who were wily in blocking his agenda and frequently planted spurious rumors about him in the media. Witnessing the incredible demands on his time inspired profound empathy in me. With his growing involvement with the boys and the principled battle he was waging, I felt a richer admiration for his abilities and the strain than I had during the congressional years.

That admiration and appreciation fueled my thinking about our future during my recuperation at the beach, looking forward to the easy way we could be with the boys, and with each other, once this time in politics was done and he could focus more of his heart and mind on our family. I guess I conveniently edited out of this vision how, as the pressures on him never let up, I saw him gradually detaching again. Mark was gone speaking or fundraising many evenings while I turned down most evening requests for the First Lady's presence so I could be with the boys. Evenings when he was in Columbia, it was routine for the staff to call to advise me where he was on his schedule. It wasn't uncommon for a staffer to call saying, "The governor wanted me to call to let you know that he has scheduled dinner for nine P.M. instead of seven because he needs time to work out before he sees the boys." I would then ask her to relay the message that dinner would be no later than eight because of bedtimes and homework. Incidents like this infuriated me. He didn't call me himself, but had an aide issuing an order from the governor's office, an order that the aide had no authority to change. Presumably neither did I.

I could see it happening again if I was honest with myself, that feeling I sometimes had when he was home from Congress that he was here, but not here. He might, in fact, already have his eye on the next goal. I could see it sometimes in the way he treated his staff. Like many people drawn to politics, most on Mark's staff believed in his mission and were willing to put up with rough treatment to serve the cause. He could be very short with the staff if he thought they'd been sloppy, wasted his time, or gone "off message."

And he was beginning to be short with me too. After the election he found himself at a disadvantage without clear continuity between the issues he campaigned on and the realities of carrying those out in office. He convinced me he needed me to help bridge that gap by helping to manage his office mornings while the boys were at school. I saw in time that my role as a sounding board and adviser had taken some of the romance out of our relationship. When he was home, I got the brunt of his complaints and his worries because I understood all the issues, and not enough of the fun-loving and patient man the public saw. Indeed, he was never short with constituents or with the man on the street, and this contrast was increasingly hard for me to endure. I tried sometimes to talk to Mark about the madness of his schedule and the damage that it was doing to us. I asked for time away, time without a political conference or family. Mark wholeheartedly agreed that we needed that time, but somehow those plans always got squeezed out by the all-important demands of his overburdened schedule.

As I recuperated at the beach that summer, I was torn between hoping Mark wouldn't run for reelection and worrying if he would be happy with the slower pace that would come with choosing to leave office. I knew in the end it would be his decision, not mine. But did he really want another four demoralizing years fighting to enact his agenda? Because of the checks and balances setup in South Carolina, he really had very little control, and it seemed he had few allies as well. Despite his high popularity statewide, the press rarely acknowledged how he stuck to his campaign principles while governing. The headlines were all, "Governor Wants Cuts in Spending" or "Sanford Bad for Public Schools." These were much more dramatic ways of phrasing what Mark was doing than "Governor does exactly what he promised to do while campaigning"!

If he decided to run again, I knew that this time I would refuse to run his campaign and stand strong against any cajoling on his part to get me to reconsider. He couldn't claim he didn't have the money to hire anyone this time. I would help out with the campaign but remove myself from any duties in his office. If we were in the governor's mansion for another four years, I decided, I would spend my time enjoying this unique life, raising our sons and instilling character, focusing on my own causes and quiet volunteer work, and planning for our family's future.

My dear friend Sally Coen joined us in New York for the convention. In our unmarked security car, we glided down Eighth Avenue, using the designated dignitary lane to pass easily through block after block of congested traffic as we made our way toward Madison Square Garden. Out the window, we could see hundreds of New Yorkers staring as the sleek black cars whisked past. As we got close to Madison Square Garden, we saw protestors and the sounds outside our windows grew louder, even if their words were indistinct. We didn't have to stop for them. We took a private route underground and pulled into a special area for VIPs.

From there, we were ushered up to a private box overlooking the convention floor, which was jammed with delegates waving flags and brightly colored banners. Sally joined us for the parties and stood with me at press events while the media hung on Mark's every word. His reputation as a man who lived by his word and didn't shrink from a fight made him a hero to some outside the state. There was some talk in the run-up to the convention about how this handsome, principled young governor might have a place on the national political stage. We knew there was a long distance between that kind of chatter and running as part of a presidential ticket, but the attention was flattering to Mark all the same. Sally was more than a little starstruck. "Wow!" she said. "I could really get used to a life like this!" I didn't want to burst her bubble by explaining how quickly it gets tiresome.

Or maybe I was just exhausted. Because of my recent surgery, I couldn't keep up with the normal frenetic schedule. Most evenings I cut out early to sleep. I now know that while I was at our friend's house resting one evening, Mark had the opportunity—and took it—to meet privately with the Argentinean woman he had met a few years earlier while in Punta del Este, Uruguay. Their reconnection, I was to learn when Mark gave an interview to the Associated Press about his affair, generated all kinds of sparks, and yet I detected nothing when he returned to me later that night.

He was able to make it all happen without me knowing and certainly without any immediate consequences from me or to his job. It's ironic that I was more deeply in love with him than I had been in a decade while he was feeling powerful, independent, and righteous in his growing success. Everything about the world around him told him he could remain immune from the consequences of meeting up with an appealing stranger for a romantic meal in a secluded New York bistro.

After the trip to New York, Mark began to consider seriously whether or not he was going to run again. He expressed real uncertainty about his strength to fight for and then serve a second term and we talked through the pros and cons at great length. We discussed carefully what would happen if he were to run and win or to run and lose, or to choose not to run and thus, in effect, hand victory over to the status quo. We also talked about the boys and what would be best for them. They wanted him to run again, both because they didn't want to see him give in and because they were enjoying their school and no longer wanted to return to Charleston. Mark decided to run this one last time.

Of course, from the moment Mark was elected in the first place his political opponents constantly called the media pushing one story or another designed to turn public opinion against him, even in tiny ways. I began to feel this political reality more once we were officially in reelection mode. I remember one particularly distasteful occasion when I agreed to help sell a new line of state pottery that had just arrived in our state gift shops. The pottery was elegant in its simplicity, made in Italy and decorated with the state logo. I allowed the state agency to include a postage-stamp-size photo of me in the sales brochure in which I was pictured drinking tea from one of the cups.

Soon after the brochure was released, a statehouse reporter called. He wanted my reaction to those who were criticizing me for my part in using state money to sell china that was not from South Carolina. I thought surely he must be kidding. I explained that I had nothing to do with the decision on where to manufacture or how to sell the china. I was merely trying to help the state make some money. He said others noted that we needed more jobs in our state and selling expensive foreign china—the cup and saucer cost $34—didn't do so.

Backed against the wall by this surprising turn of events and with Mark in a reelection campaign, I had to defend myself. I responded that the former administration used a good deal of state money to buy china and French flatware for use in the mansion. That hadn't created jobs in our state either. We even told this reporter of copies of the purchase logs for more than $100,000 worth of china and Christofle flatware. None of what we told him was in his story.

As with so many reporters, he knew the angle he wanted to take and the story would run as he wanted it to, whether honest and ethical in my view or not. This is exactly the kind of thing Mark had to deal with constantly, and I certainly didn't envy him that. It's amazing to me what sort of contortions we needed to go through to rebut this ridiculous phantom of a story. It didn't feel good to feed information to the press that might be damning to someone else's character, especially when they too had done nothing wrong. Yet I knew there were likely plenty in our state who might read such an article on the china and take their reaction to the polls against Mark.

That's the press, though: Frequently there when you don't want them around and rarely there when you do. I wish I had had the presence of mind to ask the press camped out at the end of my drive after Mark's return from Argentina where they had been for my many speeches, press conferences, or events on health, the cause I have promoted as First Lady. As a family, we did runs and walks and biked across the state and kayaked rivers to highlight the need for more regular exercise in our sedentary state, often with little notice. On one such bike ride in Aiken with a pack of other bicycle enthusiasts, I was saddened that there was almost no press to help us highlight this obvious social problem. Sadly, this is not unique to me or to South Carolina; it is all too common everywhere.

On Sunday of our last weekend before the gubernatorial reelection in November 2006, we attended the groundbreaking for the City of Light, a large Christian evangelical center that Mark had helped bring to South Carolina. Mark was on a stage adjacent to a big dirt pit full of bulldozers with other speakers and performers, some wearing sunglasses because of the bright industrial lights focused on them. The boys and I sat in the second row watching Mark give a speech that was broadcast across the globe.

Afterward, Mark said his face felt sunburned. In the middle of the night, I woke up to him sobbing next to me, his body shaking from pain. He said he couldn't open his eyes. I called an ophthalmologist friend in Charleston, even though it was two in the morning. He said it was likely that faulty lights at the event that afternoon had burned Mark's corneas. He found an all-night pharmacy in Columbia that carried the drops Mark needed. I sent security to get them and stayed up all night putting drops in Mark's eyes each hour to help soothe the pain.

In the morning Mark was taken by his security detail to the doctor. I had arranged for the boys to skip school so we could fly around the state on our last media tour before election day. We did so without Mark. Thus we entered our final election day with Mark out of commission because he had been blinded at an event about faith!

Mark met the boys and me on Sullivan's Island Monday night. He could see, but his eyes were quite swollen. I continued to put drops in his eyes through the night. Tuesday morning we all went together to cast our votes for Mark at our home precinct, but because Mark had with him only his driver's license, which had a Columbia address, and no registration card, a woman in charge there wouldn't let Mark vote. Clearly either she was not his biggest fan or she was a real stickler for rules. By this time I was thinking *Lord, what are you telling us? Is this a sign of things to come?* But any foreboding I might have felt passed quickly. Off we went to North Charleston, half an hour away, to get the appropriate documents before returning to vote and then heading to Greenville and finally Columbia to meet more family, friends, employees, and volunteers for what would turn out to be a celebration of Mark's having won another four years in office.

Mark again decided not to have a formal Inaugural Ball because the state was still in tight times, but the Republican Party paid for one as a fundraiser. In keeping with the austerity of the times, Mark chose not to wear a tuxedo, ever mindful of the image presented on camera to the general public. To match him in style and in spirit, I wore a pretty dress I borrowed from my sister-in-law Julia and a few pieces of my sister Kathy's jewelry. Even with these pared-back events, every bedroom in the mansion was filled with family, and overflow family and close friends were all in nearby hotels. There was activity everywhere and excitement in the air.

I woke on the morning of the reception to find that our dogs Jeep and Julius had discovered the packages of linens for the event that night and for the brunch the following morning and had chewed them up and strewn the remnants all across the great lawn. Surely life in this house was never dull! The party had to go on regardless of the dogs and their antics. I gathered the linens and hurried back into the house to see if we could quickly wash and press the ones the dogs had not torn and perhaps find others to make up the difference. We did, and the parties went on, with the rescued linen for the next morning safely locked away overnight.

At the second inaugural morning prayer service, our friend and pastor Greg Surratt's sermon was more than prescient in light of what has happened in the last year. Greg remarked that we will all be remembered for something and the only question that remains to be answered is, for what? He counseled Mark to remain focused in his last years of public service, as did the Old Testament character Joshua, who concentrated on serving the Lord. He urged Mark to "be strong and courageous" (Joshua 1:6) and to finish strong by remaining humble and listening to others while continuing to act on his convictions. He reminded us all that while Joshua wasn't perfect (and none of us are), Joshua didn't succumb to the selfishness and scandals of other leaders of his time. Joshua had finished well.

Mark's inaugural address was about a time for vision, and he spoke of the struggles he had faced in his first term, saying, "I stand before you a little grayer, a little wiser and tempered by reality, but nevertheless affirmed by my conviction that we can, together as South Carolinians, make a change for the better." After he took the oath, four Air National Guard F-16s flew overhead, leaving a trail of noise and smoke in the clear blue sky.

Once again we shook hands for hours as the public visited the mansion and the boys played with friends and cousins on the lawn. This time when we prepared for the barbeque at the fairgrounds we knew our way around a house that was now almost our real home. It was a joyous and happy occasion on so many levels. Instead of worrying about things to coordinate and organize, this time, I remember thinking that I should enjoy every minute I could.

ELEVEN

While I had expected Mark to slow down in his second term (at the very least the fundraising would taper off) his pace quickened instead. I suppose he didn't really take in Pastor Greg's sermon advising him to make sure every action he undertook reflected the legacy he wanted to leave. I knew, of course, that his days would be packed with state responsibilities, but I didn't expect him to take on even more. Almost from the moment of his inaugural, I saw him committing to fundraisers for the Republican Party, if not for himself, to help enact his agenda for reform. Mark began to give speeches around the country and to be courted by national conservative organizations and the national press. His restlessness was evident again. What would he do when *this* term was up?

Could he be satisfied returning to real estate? Should he run for another office?

Perhaps this is how our lives together started to twist out of balance. Our fundamental differences in pace probably should have worried me years before when I saw the lists of his goals. Instead, I believed the difference between Mark's desire for immediate success and my sense of the story of our lives spooling out over time would balance each other out. I could take the long view, and he would specialize in the here and now.

For a very long time, my marriage to Mark and our commitment to our family has allowed me to work toward my goals daily, even as true balance often eludes us. A woman's life is a juggling act, to be sure, and I'm not the only mother who feels that whatever you devote your time to this moment cheats someone else. Every day requires recalibration. Today it is Landon's turn for attention because he is graduating, while tomorrow it might be Marshall because of his tennis match. Whoever gets sick gets my time, but next week might take me away from the boys to travel with Mark or this evening might find me away from all of them for a First Lady event.

In that way, our life is kind of like a seesaw: The up and down is the only predictable part, and each one of us clusters on one side to bring some equilibrium back to the one who is flying high. What keeps me sane is the knowledge that over time the attention we all get will even out. The fact that no two days are ever the same with kids in tow has stretched me to my limits, most times happily so, but I've had faith that the priority I've given our boys will pay dividends through *their* good character and their happiness. I've trusted that Mark and I would one day have time alone again together and have drawn strength and a sense of calm from having this long-term sense of achieving goals and shared values.

I think it's fair to say that Mark has not felt this peace or this calm. Mark has always scanned the horizon for fresh opportunities and grander ways to achieve his goals. Honestly, when we met, I loved him for this too. I had lived briefly in that world of short-term goals and immediate gratification at Lazard. I understood the attraction of creating a rare opportunity and running at it with everything you had. Mark's unrelenting drive was attractive to me, given that it was married with what I thought of as a more soulful and humble character.

But Mark's anxiousness was even evident when he scheduled vacations. After Mark won reelection, we realized that we had spent so many years campaigning in some manner or another, we had never taken the boys on a spring break vacation. Mark set about making up for lost time, making plans for a one-week family adventure out West. After surfing on Laguna Beach, we toured the sights in LA and then traveled east to the Kelso Dunes and the Hoover Dam before the highlight, hiking the Grand Canyon. This was one of the prettiest hikes and one of the most enjoyable adventures we had ever shared together. In true Mark Sanford form, however, it wasn't just a mild hike. We hiked to the bottom to spend the night, then swam in the cold river before hiking back out the next morning. Then we drove to Las Vegas for an overnight and early departure the next morning. In Vegas, Mark and the boys went out on the town, touring the sights of the strip. I chose to have a glass of wine at the bar and went to bed.

That glass of wine and time alone were essential for me after all we had jammed into the previous days together, just as continuing to go, go, go was what Mark and the boys needed. I knew that if I had tried to keep them in the hotel room for some quiet time with me, it would have been Five Bulls In A Hotel Room. A boy's balance, and Mark's balance as well I supposed, is like a gyroscope; he has to keep spinning to feel calm at the center. My hope was that over time I could help my sons see that there is also value in a quieter life, the one that I was yearning for daily.

I began the summer of 2008 at the beach with the boys, as usual, while Mark finished off state business in Columbia. In late June, he went on a business trip to South America with the state's commerce department, and as I later came to learn, he completed the trip with a rendezvous with the woman he knew in Argentina. After his return, we spent a busy two weeks of work and fun at Coosaw, though I shiver when I think that while I was cleaning up after a delicious family meal with the boys and their cousins, he was emailing his "soul mate" with visions of her tan lines.

Mark had booked the entire summer with not a moment to rest. We traveled to New York City and then to Philadelphia with other governors and their families, taking a detour to visit Gettysburg. Then we were off to the Far East with the boys. In China, we met with dignitaries, including a formal Chinese lunch with our old friend Madame Wu Yi. We toured the sights in Beijing before heading west by train to visit Tibet and the base camp of Mt. Everest, followed by two days in India, a day in Bangkok, and a day in Hong Kong. We packed plenty into this whirlwind trip, and the boys returned with all sorts of rocks from their visits, but Blake somehow left his beloved Blankie Bear in Beijing. Aside from the frenetic pace, nothing Mark did during that trip hinted that his heart and mind were elsewhere engaged.

But when home that fall, I began to notice changes in Mark, a distracted quality; he didn't slow down. He began to travel to hunt on any free day, even during the week. He stopped reprimanding the boys when they acted out of line or spoke rudely to me or to others. This was a break from his previous stern approach to everything from dishonesty to back talk. As I watched him pull back from this practice, the boys took more liberties as they saw their boundaries disappear.

I found this incredibly frustrating, but he ignored me when I pointed out the change and he ignored my pleas for assistance. Instead, he began to advocate a much softer approach. "Let's just love them," he might say, as he continued to indulge their limit-pushing. He also scaled back his devotion time with the boys. This, too, frustrated me, as he was becoming in many ways as detached from the family as he had been while he was away in Congress.

I decided not to call him too harshly on the changes I saw in him, thinking he was going through another period of searching. I knew that the approaching big birthday—when he would turn fifty—was weighing on his mind and that things would return to normal as he came to terms with that milestone.

They did not. We hosted receptions for supporters at the mansion but sadly, he still sometimes asked, "Who are my friends?" I pointed out the friends we had hosted as guests at football games, invited for overnights at the mansion or weekends at Coosaw. These were people who were truly fond of him as a person as well as supportive of his agenda. But he was right to notice that he didn't have a group of close friends—at least not that he had kept up with or met with regularly—that would keep him accountable and down to earth. As rich as our life may have seemed to an outsider, in some ways, Mark's life in politics has made for a lonely existence for all of us, especially given the isolated nature of the compound on which we lived in Columbia. I understand how he had become so compartmentalized and walled off from real understanding of his friendships and their value. With Mark as governor, we were often so busy that we saw very little of the kind of people who knew us well and would always be brave enough to hold us accountable for our actions. Friends share a healthy respect for one another and their similarities, differences, strengths, and weaknesses. In this crush of people who wanted to be friends with us for their own reasons, many valid, I found myself starved for real friendship. Many of our true friends were reluctant to call us because they assumed we were busy. I would often learn, after the fact, that they had been in Columbia for, say, a child's soccer game and stayed in a hotel, not wanting to bother me. All I wanted was the company of real friends instead of the tiresome busyness and loneliness that came with the job and the house. I began to encourage friends to please call when they were in Columbia. I told them I would honestly let them know if we were busy or not. Some were better at staying in touch when in town than others, but all had great intentions and remain close today. In time, I also made great friends in Columbia for all the right reasons, as did our boys. But for Mark it has seemed loneliest.

Indeed, he spent most of his time asking others for help with his campaign or pushing an issue and seemed to spend little time reassessing himself and whether he was living life according to the goals and values he held dear. Though always for good causes, charity dinners and political events can't replace casual, unstructured, let-down-your-guard time with old and dear friends.

Though I wouldn't have thought anyone could take much more than Mark was already juggling, in the fall, the pressures on him increased dramatically. The economy in our state soured, and then the national markets collapsed. Mark traveled to hearings on Capitol Hill to speak. He stood firmly against the stimulus package that President Obama and others promoted as the solution to our financial crisis. When he was fighting to reject federal stimulus money in early 2009, the bulk of the political class and the media and a large majority in the public couldn't conceive of someone being against so-called "free" money, even as his popularity with conservatives was incredibly high.

From late 2008 to June 2009 Mark did somewhere close to eighty national interviews on the stimulus and government spending, an astonishing number. The more outspoken he was, the more the press wanted him on air. People began to call or write from all over the country urging Mark to consider running for president in 2012 and, regardless, to continue to fight Obama and the huge increase in spending. Our country needed him, they said, and he was eager to rise to the occasion. Whether with adulation or criticism, the media attention that came with his position and notoriety fueled both his belief in his convictions and, I now see, his ability to compartmentalize his emotional response to it all. Wrapped up in staying true to his message, he became empty of connection to almost everything else.

Mark and I traveled to Miami for a Republican Governors Association conference in November 2008, where he was elected chairman of that organization. Shortly thereafter, he traveled to Ireland to shoot birds with other RGA contacts. At the end of the trip to Ireland, he disappeared. He had stopped calling home, and I called his staff to find out what was going on. They said he had flown to New York, but they were unclear on the purpose of the visit. I didn't know either, but I would soon come to know that this trip to New York was for a rendezvous with his mistress. When he finally called, I asked him what he was doing in New York and who he was with. He told me he was alone. I said that I didn't believe him. The pressure had been getting to him, he said, and, unbelievably, he was also upset about the bald spot that was forming at the back of his head. He just needed some time away from all of the stress and his worries. I cut him some slack. I can't say I completely bought the line he was selling me, but I put the unaccounted-for time out of my head. I chose to ignore my doubts.

In any event, I had plenty of reasons to appreciate the pressures he was under, pressures that seemed to mount every day. In December 2008, Mark and his staff worked long hours trying to finish the budget for the next fiscal year. The state revenues were down substantially. Mark came home drained every night, telling me of the awful choices he had to make on the budget, where each proposed cut was as difficult as the next and every one of them slashed at something that had already been cut to the bone. Though the legislators held the power, the governor led with his budget, and he would take most of the blame. Every possible moment he was not needed at the office, he seemed to be on the television or away at a new hunting spot or traveling to give a speech or raising RGA funds or money for his own cause. When he was home, he was often speaking on the local or national news before dinner, sometimes returning to a television studio to appear again on the late-night news cycle. His frantic schedule coupled with his frenetic drive to fill every minute as well as his unquenchable ambition were all tearing him apart. He looked exhausted and had bags under his eyes; he had lost weight and his eyes appeared glazed. It seemed to me that Mark had become the empty-eyed politician he used to abhor.

All of these dramatic changes in him suggested a deep emptiness inside, too. Even a young body needs time to rest, to recharge, but all Mark did was charge ahead, ignoring how his worst fears about aging were manifesting in his body. Mark has long had trouble with his back and has suffered a sore shoulder from time to time, but that fall it seemed as though his body was completely falling apart as he clung desperately to the desires of youth. It was apparent that he was suffering. The yogis refer to suffering, or dhukha, as the resistance or reaction to pain. When I looked at Mark, I saw a man in so much pain: physical, intellectual, and emotional. Somewhere inside of me I knew he was in moral conflict as well, but that was honestly something I chose not to explore. My concern and my pleas for him to slow down, to soften, went unheard. There was so much on the surface that seemed to need my attention, that the idea of scratching that surface and confronting Mark with what I saw was just not tenable.

On one level, you might say that Mark was having a classic midlife crisis. Yet to label it as such, pack it neatly in a box, and place it on a shelf denies the way his adherence to political principle, the public acclaim, government pressure, and media attention aided and abetted this episode. Of course, he had the tendency to view his life as a quest that was never completed, and this would have existed within him even if he had never been elected. In a way that is just what drives him. I can see Mark's break with his values now as probably a combination of these forces: the unreal way in which being a public figure distorted his sense of self compounded by the coming crisis that was turning fifty.

Mark had long lived in a world where he never had to perform the normal tasks of life nor suffer the consequences of his lapses of decorum in the office or spikes of bad temper, albeit often with a gentle voice. No matter his private failings, his staff protected him from exposure. But now, the media, the hated media, was lavishing positive attention on him, and he found it irresistible. He was the man of the moment, the stalwart hero who was standing on principle and refusing to accept money from the federal government. In all ways, he was a man who stood apart from the quotidian world. He was lauded, celebrated for his constant seeking of new ideas, new horizons, and, unbeknownst to me, new sensations. Was it so much of a stretch then for him to think that if he worked hard enough at it, he might beat this aging thing too?

Here again, our difference in approach is profound. I have always looked forward to getting older. As someone who has dozens of things to do on any given day, or at a particular moment, I expect that when I reach my senior years all of that will gracefully, gently subside. As each year passes, I feel more and more content with who I am and how I have lived my life. As my body began to slowly age (I too have had health and age-related issues, including many skin cancer scares and many minor surgeries to remove them), I was more and more awake to the precious gifts surrounding me each day, but Mark's angst was growing about what was to come. Where I was learning to accept gracefully the challenges that have come with aging, he had tried to deny them. As he faced the prospect of turning fifty and his time as governor was coming to an end, Mark continued to live in an increased frenzy, as if something were missing and he had to find it before he died.

Perhaps the foundation for the differences in Mark and my approaches to aging is the fact that all four of my grandparents were still alive when I was a child. Mark briefly knew two of his grandparents, but perhaps he never saw the beauty or wisdom in their age. My mom's parents, Honey and Bumpa, were full of fun and energetic almost until they died. Bumpa was tall and bright and could make me laugh. I remember sitting on his lap as he blew smoke rings from his pipe. His other classic grandfather trick was making a silver dollar magically appear from behind my ear. Naturally, he let me keep the silver dollar, making it that much more special. Honey, my grandmother, is my real model for aging well. In many ways, she blossomed as she aged. She was soft-spoken, petite, and graceful, and her grace increased in her later years. She walked daily, stretched her mind by reading, and even took up painting late in life.

My father's parents showed me a different advantage to the later stages of life. My Gramps awed me with his wisdom about business and his insights into character. Older people have so much time—time to listen, reflect, and share magical memories. All my grandparents had experienced great joys and successes, as well as tribulations, but they had reached a state of contentment and enjoyment. With them as my examples, I had never been fearful about aging, recalling John Greenleaf Whittier's lines: "Strike when thou wilt the hour of rest,/But let my last days be my best." The family did our part to make the elders feel as if their last days were indeed their best. We celebrated milestones in our grandparents' lives, such as birthdays and fiftieth anniversaries, and we always welcomed opportunities to be with them.

Anne Morrow Lindbergh said, "only in growth, reform, and change, paradoxically enough is true security to be found." When I think of those words, I recall how gracefully Honey lived after Bumpa died. She could have withered at the prospect of living her last years alone. Her security came from living in the present. I see the same quality in my mother as I have watched her play tennis, paint, and enjoy time with her grandchildren, living far longer than any doctor projected. I am reminded of how special each day of life is and how important it is to seek to enjoy each step along the way. As with meditation in yoga, I am mindful that I need to learn to become present and familiar with myself so I can feel my experiences and not just react to them.

As I felt myself happily relaxing into my age, I was pulling away from Mark's world. Weekends at Coosaw and time at our beach house have helped balance the demands on our time while in Columbia, and we have all cherished these getaways. I think the boys and Mark have been most happy at Coosaw, where they could just be boys, kayaking the rivers or creeks or swimming to the banks of pluff mud at low tide. Mark is the Pied Piper there, able to round up all the children and get them working on some big project.

Some weekends he rented a track hoe, and he and the boys replaced a floodgate or repaired dikes. Other times all of them, even the little guys, took to the woods to set a big fire—a controlled burn—to cut back the underbrush. I didn't fully partake of these manly events but I often watched for a while. I enjoyed the peace of walking at Coosaw, finding balance on the shifting terrain. Uncluttered time in nature has been my personal time to recharge, and then I rejoin the noisy men. I relish the delight on the boys' faces as they return covered in soot or mud, hungry for a hearty meal I have cooked, followed by discussion around the fire after dinner or a Jeep ride under the stars to spot deer in the woods. My eyes were trained on the horizon too, but my vision of it was us at the beach, Mark at home, while we as a couple cherished the launching of our four fine young men into the world. As Henri Bergson said, "To exist is to change, to change is to mature, to mature is to go on creating oneself endlessly." As I faced the realities of my aging and dealt with my various health crises, I wanted to grow to understand them, to deal with them, to learn from them, and to live wholly with them.

We had lived our time in the public eye, but my vision of our future as we grew older was one where we could be as vital to the world around us in a much more private context. I was moving inward, slowing down, reveling in these changes and the changes to come. Little did I understand, as I started to draw more strongly on my inner life and look toward my goals, that January would bring me a revelation that would derail that strong vision I had of my years to come with my family as I knew it.

TWELVE

I always believed that Mark and I had no secrets. After all of these years in the public eye, our lives were open books to one another, let alone to the public. Though we drifted apart a bit during his time as governor, we were partners in parenting, and we were still intimate. The physical space we shared even remained close: In the office adjacent to our bedroom in the governor's mansion, our desks were next to each other. So it was not at all odd on an afternoon back in January for me to be looking in his desk.

The beginning of the year is the time I put things to right after the holidays. Mark's State of the State speech and the Obama inauguration had already taken up catch-up time but with Mark away hunting Thursday and Friday that week, I had the time to tackle a few lingering issues. One of them was to search for some documents I thought would settle a question about Coosaw that had come up between Mark and his siblings. While the boys were at school on Friday, I searched the files we kept in storage but didn't find what I was looking for there. Later that day, it occurred to me that Mark's desk might hold the needed paperwork. If what I was looking for wasn't there, I told myself, I'd call it quits and let Mark search further himself when he got home.

I walked into the tall office with long windows overlooking the mansion driveway and went to Mark's desk. Ignoring the scattered papers on top and the stacks of books on the floor that Mark planned to read, I went straight for the drawer on the left side, where I knew Mark kept files about current issues. In random order, one labeled simply "B" caught my eye. I opened it and saw quickly that this was not a file dedicated, as I thought, to correspondence with Mark's brother Bill—often called just B by his siblings. Instead, a letter, an article clipped from a magazine, and a printed email exchange inside told me that B stood for Belen, a woman, I learned sitting there, Mark had slept with and whom he believed to be his eternal love.

I suppose it's cliché to say that I felt as if I had been punched in the gut. But that's the best description I can muster for what this surprise felt like. I was short of breath. I began to shake. Stunned, I wasn't sure of what to do next. I had so many questions. How could I not have known? Had I really known, on some level? When and where had he been seeing her? How had he found time for an affair? Did he really love her? How could he do this to me and to the boys? I read the letter again and saw the depth of what he professed to be his feeling. I looked at the article, but it didn't mean anything to me; for all I know even today, it may have been misfiled.

The email made things still more clear. It showed Mark had arranged to use a friend's apartment in New York City for a visit he had scheduled in the coming weeks. I knew that the ostensible reason for the trip was to meet with publishers interested in his idea for a book on conservative values, but I could only assume he was also planning to see his lover then. He had been gone so much recently . . . where had he actually been? I don't know how long I sat in his chair. Eventually I got up and moved to my side of the office and sat motionless at my desk a bit longer, the thin file in my lap. I tried to think of what I should do. Should I call him? Should I call a friend? A lawyer? Should I cry? Was this even happening? I was shocked into stillness, until I heard Mark's voice downstairs.

I put the file on my desk and stood up when he walked into our office. Fresh from the hunt, he was disheveled, and his plaid shirt was untucked. He looked as if he hadn't slept all night. He kissed me hello and then went to his desk. Still dumbstruck, I calmly handed him the letter and confronted him very simply with what I'd discovered: "Please tell me about this."

Mark glanced down at the letter, and his shoulders slumped immediately. Again I noticed that he looked very tired. "Jenny, I'm sorry. I'll end it," he said.

The next thing I said had been looping endlessly through my mind and seemed to be what mattered most of all: "Well, do you love her?"

"No," he said emphatically. Despite his declaration of love in the letter, I believed him. "She doesn't mean anything. In fact I was up really late last night telling Jim Kuyk that this was crazy and that I had to end it." Jim is an old friend—he was in our wedding, in fact—and Mark's lawyer. I didn't think there was any legal significance in Mark's having confided in him, but I wondered immediately how many people knew about this affair before I did.

We heard the sound of a few of the boys running up the stairs to greet Mark.

"Let's finish this discussion downstairs," Mark said and then turned to his sons and tousled heads and caught them up on his successful hunt. I would have given anything for this to be a discussion that had an end point, but I suspected it wasn't something we could dispense with simply "downstairs." Still, downstairs I went.

A few minutes later, boys scattered to other parts of the house, Mark and I sat together on a couch in the library. I sobbed softly—still unable or unwilling, I'm not sure which, to rant and rave with the hurt I was feeling—as Mark tried to explain himself. I was hoping it was just a one-time event, an act of passion, but Mark admitted that he had seen this woman in Argentina and then twice in New York. I asked if there had been other affairs and he insisted that this was his only transgression, the only one. Insisting Belen didn't mean anything to him and avoiding any real details of the logistics of their time together, Mark promised to end the affair. His voice was kind and apologetic but he didn't reach out to comfort me. A profound sadness came over me sitting there. A fundamental part of what I believed about my husband and about our life together had just died and it seemed as though I might never get it back.

My mind raced, looking for an explanation better than the one he was providing. Mark had abstained from sex and drinking during college while his dad was so sick. Having gotten a few things out of my own system in college, I could appreciate that he had long wondered what, if anything, he had missed by not experimenting in those years. I knew that he was under almost impossible pressure on the job. I understood how something like this might have happened theoretically, though I couldn't wrap my head around how Mark—this man of his word and of faith—could have made such terrible choices. Still, I knew that I could and would forgive him. It might have been my survival instinct kicking in, a willingness to forgive and move on, perhaps even the hope that in forgiving quickly I could eradicate the ugly knowledge I'd gained that day. But my immediate impulse to forgive Mark has not proven to be only that. I can see now that forgiving him was an essential part of healing for myself as well.

Through tears, I told Mark that I wanted to forgive him and to believe that this was it, that it wouldn't ever happen again. My simple condition was that he had to fully commit to the marriage in a way that he had not done in the past. It had to be better, not just a return to the same. Still sitting apart from me—perhaps a posture that should have worried me—he agreed.

At dinner that night, I tried to keep up the normal patter for the boys' sake, but I left the table early, explaining that I simply wasn't feeling well. I sobbed upstairs in my bathroom. I don't know how long I sat there, but at some point in the evening Mark came in, hugged me gently, and assured me everything was going to be okay. How I wanted to believe that! What a wonderful thing it would have been to just believe that and try to move on. But as anyone who has ever been betrayed knows, we can't really outsmart or overrule the part of the brain that has registered that betrayal.

Forgiveness, too, is a willful and deliberate act and it takes such effort. I made the effort, but I lost sleep over it. For many nights—and many months—I often had trouble getting to sleep and had a terrible time staying that way. I often got up in the wee hours of the morning, read my Bible, and stared into space. I began to keep a journal of my thoughts and some of Mark's comments and found that doing so helped me focus on what mattered. I was beat down, exhausted, and deeply sad, but the first thing I wrote in that journal shows me that even in that dark hour I was determined to continue to see my glass as half full. I started with Psalm 118:24 "This is the day the Lord has made, let us rejoice and be glad in it."

The next day, Saturday, Mark and I were scheduled to attend a black-tie dinner in Charleston. Ostensibly to get ready, but really just to clear my head, I went out for a pedicure and a massage, soaking up every minute of the solitude. Discovering Mark's affair had somehow made me feel ugly, unwanted, and even dirty. For just a little while, the pampering and the fancy dress I put on that evening made me feel good.

I asked Mark to drive instead of taking a security detail to the event so we could speak frankly during the hours in the car. As we talked, it became clear to me that, contrary to what he'd said the day before, Mark had real feelings for this woman. He touted her wealth, bristled when I asked questions, and defended her when I referred to her plainly as his "whore." "She is not a whore!" he protested. He seemed to be oblivious to his ability to pierce my heart.

We also spoke of the trip to the world economic forum in Davos, Switzerland, where we were scheduled to go the next day. I told Mark that I didn't see how going to Davos could be a priority at this time. Instead, I thought we should stay home and we should be together without other people, or dinners or speeches. Mark resisted upending our plans, but he ultimately agreed we would stay home and even go away together for a weekend.

A few days later, I asked Mark if he had told Belen that their affair was over. He said that doing so wouldn't be quite that easy. Though I had understood that they had got together while Mark was on a commerce department trip to Argentina in June 2008, their relationship, he explained, had actually started—albeit platonically—seven years earlier via email. She had been a friend, and he didn't think he could just cut her off so quickly. He still hoped he could travel to New York in a few weeks to see her. He promised he would end it there in person. I wouldn't have it—he had to end it immediately on the phone.

It was Wednesday before Mark emailed Belen to ask her to call so they could talk about ending the affair. He spoke to her from his office for I don't know how long. I didn't want to know; I also didn't need to know that he had found the call difficult, but he told me it was. But difficult or not, tears or no tears, afterward he told me unequivocally that the affair was over. I felt relieved, to be sure. But I knew that the flesh and the spirit can lust against one another and I worried that what he had originally said might be true: It might not be so easy to end this thing.

I had long since realized that marriage to Mark was not going to be all roses or romance. Certainly I didn't always feel loved by him or have that "in-love" feeling for him as often as I would have liked, but that, I rationalized—and believed—was real marriage. I had faith that we had a *real* marriage, one that could weather the periods of distance and come back again to connection. Our stresses were real but were focused in an honorable direction. My daily prayers had always included prayers for my marriage. After finding that letter, I needed God's love and grace even more powerfully.

As we'd planned when we cancelled the trip to Switzerland, we traveled that weekend to the mountains around Asheville without the boys. This was meant to be a time to reconnect but it'd been such a long time since we'd made this space for each other that it was more surreal than relaxing. Plus, the circumstances surrounding our decision to be alone now hung over us the whole time. At some point over that weekend I realized that I had just begun an emotional roller-coaster ride, one that would last far longer than I could ever have imagined. Just because we agreed we would put Mark's affair behind us didn't mean we could do so quickly. That recognition was a blow as well.

And, of course, it wasn't yet over. That weekend, Mark broke down and cried, but not for what I expected might bring him to tears. He explained that he had always been so *good*, so dutiful. He had led his siblings through a tough time after their father died. He had remained true to his conservative principles in his political career although doing so meant going against a considerable tide. It became clear to me this romantic relationship he had was a way of doing something for himself—it felt good and he didn't really want to give it up. Though on that weekend away he didn't spell it out explicitly, it was becoming clear that he intended to see her again in New York.

How could he possibly think I would let him go through with the plan I had seen him make in that email, a plan to spend two nights in New York with her? I asked incredulously. I told him repeatedly that I felt it was one thing to forgive adultery but in no way could I condone it, especially in my own marriage. I wrestled with this very thing in my journal that night: "I trust his intentions are good—he says it is over—but how can I trust the result when faced with such temptation? And what of the lack of humility? The lack of respect for me? Is he not putting her feelings over mine? Does he really love me?" I felt so sad and misunderstood. Though forgiveness might be possible, it dawned on me that reconciliation would be a harder thing to manage. I wondered constantly, frantically searching my heart to know if the right reaction was to leave him.

Faith requires prayer and time, and I suspected Mark's prayers had been neglected given the demands on his time. The world around us conspires to make finding time for prayer difficult. A well-known Psalm says "Be still and know that I am God." In *A Gift from the Sea,* Anne Morrow Lindbergh also talks of the importance of seeking solitude amidst our multitasking lives. She speaks of the importance of finding empty space—because, as she puts it, our time is all used up or scribbled on. It is in this empty space, or when we can be still, that we find God and reconnect with our true inner self. My sense of security for our marriage came from a deep well of understanding of ebb and flow, a concept that honored commitment over the long haul and was founded in my faith. In accepting our distance as an inevitable part of eventually coming back together, I had settled into a peace with our life and lifestyle with the help of my prayers.

In retrospect, I might have been learning to justify Mark's lack of empathy, his travels and schedule, or other imperfections. I now wonder if he took our stated certainty of a future together as a license to stray without consequence. But all this is even still just speculation on my part, and in those early days it was far too much for me to even begin to consider. The questions that dogged me were ones that would ultimately break the commitment from my side as well: At what point are children ill-served by the example set by their parents and their marriage? And what of my personal dignity and self-respect if Mark continued to see his lover?

Later in the year, when I'd confided in friends about what was happening and what Mark was asking to do, I better understood that allowing him to see Belen in New York—which is what I eventually agreed to let him do—was ludicrous. Of course, it was ludicrous of him to continue to ask me to let him go, but he wore me down, asking again and again and insisting that the way for this to be over was to allow him the closure he needed. Even stranger—though a lifeline to me at the time—was our agreement that we would ask for a friend's help in keeping Mark in line.

Every minute of Mark's two days in New York—including meetings with publishers—he would have a friend of ours, Cubby Culbertson, by his side. Mark could see Belen for dinner with Cubby as their escort. Cubby had been and still is a dear friend to both of us, and he was helping Mark regain his moral focus from the moment I learned of the infidelity. He stepped up and into this odd request, dropping his own plans to help an old friend stay the course and save his marriage. His willingness to help Mark and me discreetly was a tremendously generous and selfless act, but I wasn't at peace with the decision before or even after the arrangements were made.

Indeed, before Cubby agreed to accompany Mark I wrote in my journal, "I cannot condone this future act because A) it is wrong in God's eyes B) it would cause me to lose my self-respect, dignity etc—esp as we look to the boys as example going forward. . . . Perhaps he needs to be thinking of how he gets back his dignity in God's eyes—by His grace."

My arm twisted into this strange position, however, Mark went to New York and Cubby went too. The first night, I received a text from Cubby that read "Sleep well. He played by the rules." I went to sleep but once again could not sleep long. Instead, I thought long and hard about whether Mark had ever loved me and about whether I should leave him. Again, I turned to my journal. I wrote: "Is M's suffering now/future because A) he will not have/see his "eternal love" or B) he hurt his wife, whom he truly loves? Can I stay in marriage if the answer is A? I know I can stay if the answer truly is B." I thought about what it would do to our boys if I left yet I also wondered if I could stay much longer if Mark didn't show real effort toward making the marriage stronger.

While Mark was gone I prayed for strength and shed many tears. I also began to be more fully aware of how out of touch I was with the demons Mark was wrestling with and that I could not really help him.

I expected or hoped that Mark would be a new man when he returned from New York but in time I saw that was not at all the case. After a few good weeks he became distant again, and before long he was pestering me for permission to see his lover that summer so he could find "the key to his heart." That he would consider asking me repeatedly for permission to see his lover again was unfathomable. It was one thing for me to forgive his indiscretions and move toward reconciliation, but to condone it further meant for me to compromise my own morals and integrity. That was a bridge too far for me and cut deeply against my faith. I have committed plenty of moral sins in my past, but in each case I have grown in the aftermath, begging forgiveness from the Lord or from others and moving on as a better person, learning from past mistakes. But this was missing with Mark. He seemed to be traveling a path of his own making, seeking his own comfort, no longer guided by a power above. I began to see him as lost, disconnected from his basic values, and I began to pray differently.

Now I prayed for His will to be done and for me to bear the future with grace and peace. I asked for calm for my boys and acceptance of the future. I sought understanding of Mark's actions and prayed that the Lord would wake him to the error of his ways. I praised more and asked less. A verse I contemplated was Nehemiah 8:10: "for this day is holy to our Lord. Do not sorrow, for the joy of the Lord is your strength." I tried over and over to put joy in my head and heart and to remain strong. I focused on the love from God, the blessings in my life—boys, family, faith, and friends.

I began to think differently about the marriage than I had

in years past too. I thought of the lies and the deception and questioned how I would know when it had all ended. I pondered humility and remorse. I read of Paul in 1 Timothy and considered how he had acknowledged his sins and become humble in that knowledge. As he matured he grew into a great leader by tapping into that humbleness. Mark's star had been rising in the political world, but I was not seeing or feeling any humility.

Even as I wrestled with what I might have seen or what I should have understood earlier, I refused to beat myself up over my past choices. I forgave myself my long-standing belief that Mark and I would be together alone again after the *next* political position. I was proud to conclude that giving and doing more for our marriage than I had received in return had been the right thing to do for our family. But, I also finally understood that our relationship couldn't be so lopsided going forward. I had told him as much that first day I confronted him: My simple condition for staying together was just that. But I seemed to reach something much more clearly identifiable as a decision, beginning while Mark was gone in New York: I could stay in the marriage if Mark found a true and humble spirit of remorse and if he recognized that he loved me and that he had deeply hurt me. What Mark did had changed the dynamics. I was committed to doing my part but I could not be the only one doing so.

I was under no illusion that Mark would change overnight, so I steeled myself to be gentle and patient. I prayed for the strength to be so. Throughout, I reminded myself that no matter what, I was loved by my God, my friends, and my family, that I was being the best I could be. This knowledge gave me some peace. I felt sanguine about my future, whatever it might turn out to hold for me.

THIRTEEN

The weekend Mark traveled to Argentina, a reporter called to ask if I knew where my husband was, and I had a choice to make. The choice was not whether to tell the truth. Like everyone in my family, I always pretty much say what I think and move on. In the world of politics, that's not always the best policy, despite my strong impulse to do so. The goal with a reporter was to reveal enough of the truth to satisfy his curiosity while saying as little of substance as possible.

Consider what I could have said. Mark was a man who spoke often about living according to principles and values, and our family was part of his appeal, evidence of character. Revealing that I had kicked him out would allow his political enemies to gleefully advance any number of agendas. Even in my heartbreak, I considered his public image almost as often as I plumbed the impulses of my heart.

Truth was, I had wanted to leave him almost as soon as he returned from his farewell trip to New York with Cubby, even if it would serve to wake him up and ultimately save the marriage and family. The begging to be allowed to see his mistress again in Argentina began shortly thereafter, and I had had about all I could take.

Mark still saw me as his sounding board. Over those months, he wondered aloud to me if he shouldn't just follow his heart. What if he could find true happiness only in Argentina? Would he always live his life in regret, in wonder, because he didn't take this chance? Clearly, these were thoughts I wished he'd kept to himself. He was in a daze, though, a dreamy state similar to the way he appeared at points in the now-famous press conference after Father's Day. Indeed, when I'd reminded him later of the hurtful things he'd said in those intervening months, he couldn't remember most of them.

There was many a time I pictured just packing up the boys and letting Mark sort it out on his own. Most in the small circle who knew my situation recommended I do just that. But that would have put the burden of halting his rising star on me, and I wasn't ready to shoulder that responsibility.

In the beginning the circle of people I confided in was indeed small. It included two friends, my sister, and Jack, who had advised me well and cooled me down after Mark rented our house out without consulting me. The day after I discovered the letter, it was actually Mark who suggested I call Jack in DC. I wanted help, I needed counsel, and I trusted Jack. As before, he was ever kind and patient, telling me emphatically not to beat myself up. He also gave me two excellent pieces of advice on that first phone call.

He knew that my instinct would be to keep this to myself. "Jenny don't do this alone," he said, urging me to confide in just one or two very close friends.

I took his advice, but I didn't feel comfortable just picking up the phone and telling this shattering news to the two women I chose to confide in: Frannie and Lalla Lee, my close friends in Charleston. Instead, I texted them, asking them to call when they could do so privately. Both called right away. We cried together and they vowed to help me through, as good friends do.

We set up time to pray together as well. Days later, when I joined them in Charleston for that purpose, I gave them the love letter I'd found. I had considered destroying it, but something told me I might need it one day as proof of the affair. I hoped that day would never come but, in the meantime, I didn't want it around our house where I might read it again. Those were emotions I was trying to move beyond. I trusted them to keep that document safe. A few weeks later, I shared the secret with my sister Gier too, and she joined in this sisterhood of support. For many long and difficult months, I was thankful to have these women ready to listen whenever I called.

Jack's other piece of advice was how to handle Mark. Jack

understood men in power well. He counseled that seeking revenge would erode any chance of reconciliation. I needed to resist the urge to rant or get back at Mark. If Mark said things that hurt or upset me, I was not to respond. Easier said than done, he agreed, but he was offering to take the burden off my shoulders. I should hand these hurts to Jack, who would confront Mark in a way that my tears might derail. This method would allow me, Jack said, to be like "the Bride of Christ." I could work on forgiveness and kindness, while he worked with Mark to make amends.

I needed Jack's tag-team support very quickly thereafter. Just a few days later, Mark was angry at me for convincing him not to go to Davos, though it was also clear that he was just plain angry with me for catching him in this entanglement in the first place. Holding my tongue and then tattling on Mark to a third party was difficult. My instinct at a moment like this was to stand up for *myself.* But I followed Jack's plan and he backed me up, explaining to Mark that traveling to Davos at a critical time like this was absolutely the wrong thing to do.

There were times when I wanted to scream and rant at Mark, and I'm sure I was snide on occasion or hurt him with the truth. For the most part, however, discussions between us did not spiral into spiteful words. I was quite disciplined. I don't think I ever said anything I felt I couldn't take back. With Jack's wise counsel, I left the punishment to someone else.

Yet Mark was unrelenting, in time escalating pressure to

get me to condone his foreign adventure. Once I realized we were going in the wrong direction, I was ready to move out. In April and early May, Jack was of the same mind. He suggested that I'd put up with too much and urged me to leave Mark as a way to wake him up and perhaps save the marriage. My female friends agreed that the shock of us gone was the best chance I had to knock some sense into Mark. But Marshall was just about to take his exams for junior year, the ones that really count for college. If I could avoid pulling the rug out from underneath him just long enough to help him get through this critical educational moment, I would.

In early May I wrote in my journal, "Allowing my husband to see his lover for whatever reason goes against who I am and my entire sense of right and wrong. I explained this over and over to Mark but he thought I was not hearing or understanding him. I understand him—he loves someone else and he wants to have one final fling with her to see if it brings 'true happiness' before he settles with me and puts his 'heart to rest' over her. What he does not see is how morally offensive it is to me to even listen to this. It is ripping my heart up and I told him so."

I was at a real crossroads. And I was very tense. I wasn't so worried about going it alone. I was worried about direction. Because of his position, I didn't want to make a rash decision that would bring down Mark's career, and he knew I cared about helping him avoid that. And I was thinking of the boys, who didn't deserve this in the least. In retrospect, I know I was probably too respectful of his work responsibilities and was letting him too much off the hook of his home responsibilities.

So we came up with a plan. The plan I favored was to throw the kids into the car on the last day of school and leave with them for the summer to a place unknown to Mark. Jack found us a house in Annapolis, where Marshall was enrolled in a one-week session at the Naval Academy. From there we would find a place somewhere on Cape Cod, and Mark would not know where to find us. Jack said this plan was what a guy like Mark really needed, some real shock to his tightly controlled self-wound world. I felt as though I was still trying to give back sight to the blinded soul.

Before school ended and we could depart in surprise, Mark continued wearing me down. I didn't like negotiating with him. He wanted my permission to go, but I was never going to grant it. Why did he persist? I explained that I thought the decision before him was if he could commit wholly to me in a way he hadn't done before. Give it a year. Give it two years. And if it doesn't work out between us, then go see her, I said. She's not going anywhere.

"What if she does?" he'd ask. "Do you want to wake up when you are eighty and know you never had a heart connection?" Fast-talking, straight-shooting me, I was largely speechless. Of course, I believed I'd had a "heart connection" with him!

Anyway, Mark got wind of my plans for leaving town and it did *not* wake him up, so I instantly changed plans. We would head to the beach on Sullivan's Island, and instead of deserting Mark, we would welcome him to come and be with us, spending time with us with no schedule whatsoever. He said he would join us at the beach during that largely unscheduled three-week period soon to come. I thought we would slowly settle into something that was better during his visit and that our open time as a family would be a salve for us all. Mark, however, did not seem happy about it all.

Instead, his yearnings for his distant lover intensified as soon as he arrived at the beach. I'd never seen him like this. He was just in a tizzy, an internal tizzy, and he couldn't sit still. He was sometimes sleepless, and I knew I didn't understand the demons he was wrestling. His requests to see his lover now were almost frantic in tone. He even asked if we could formally separate for one week so his visit would be legally permissible. Needless to say, that was not even a bit okay with me. When I wouldn't budge, he began calling friends seeking their permission. Why permission from a friend would have mattered, I don't know. But none of his friends told him that they thought this was a good idea.

On Mark's second night with us at the beach, we went to a good friend's house for dinner. I found it too much for me to bear being there as the married couple managing our children with smiles on our faces when there was so much roiling beneath the surface. I left early on my bike.

Once home alone, I sat on the porch looking at the sea, waiting for some kind of an answer to come to me. For months, I had been holding this secret for him. Although I had called a lawyer shortly after I learned of the affair to see how one prepared for divorce, I had not filed any formal documents or successfully used legal leverage out of respect for him and his position. In early May, however, I had tried: I had had my lawyer draw up a contract saying I would not tell anyone else of the affair out of respect for his political career if he would agree not to see Belen. He would not sign the contract. Later in May, I had told our political adviser of the situation, shocking him completely. He wrote Mark an impassioned email warning him that if he didn't reverse course, "you will lose your wife, your children, and your career." I also told my assistant of the affair and of my struggles to wake him up. As more people learned of the affair, the likelihood it would become publicly known also increased.

I was up at three in the morning sitting on the porch looking out at the ocean when Mark came to sit with me.

"What's wrong?" he asked.

"What do you think is wrong? I'm married to a guy who is in love with someone else," I said. "I'm not going to stay in a marriage like that."

"No, no, I love you," he said.

"Then why do you want to go see her?" I asked.

"It's my heart. I've got to figure this thing out."

Once again, the inanity and insensitivity of his remark left me reeling. No one has the key to your heart, I explained. *You* have the key to your heart. Yet again I was clear: "I will not allow you to go see her," I said.

In his continued misery, I heard his decision. I had had enough. I told him he had to leave the house that day and not contact me or the boys. My hope was that starving him of daily contact with me and the boys might bring him around to appreciate what he might lose.

About nine later that morning, we called the boys into the family room and sat them down. "You know your mom and I have been having some problems," Mark began. "You've seen our strains and you've seen your mom crying. I haven't been good to her. I'm mixed up right now and I've got to get myself right. I'm going to be leaving for a month. I'm not going to talk to you for thirty days, until July 10. I'm just going to go write my book and get my head right." The boys were upset and started to object, but ultimately they accepted that we were serious.

I walked with Mark out to the driveway. I told him, "You look me in the eye and tell me you will not see her."

"I will not see her," he said. He had always prided himself on his honesty.

"You mean it?"

"I will not see her," he said, before departing with security for Columbia.

Apparently, within a few hours, he bought his ticket to Argentina.

Although I had been running the household alone for more than a decade, the space left by Mark's departure was unsettling. Before, I always had a sense of Mark as the vital missing piece. During my days with the boys when he was traveling and working, I thought often about where he was and the important work he was doing for the state or nation. Thinking about what he was doing filled my mind with purpose, somehow making my loneliness easier. Now, without him calling frequently to make plans or consult with me about news of the day, the world shifted. I started to understand what life would be like without Mark, and it was amazing how quickly I became comfortable with the idea of it.

I knew he was in the Capitol the week after he left us at the beach, and I also know a few of his close friends went to be with him to berate him for thinking of going to see his mistress. Mark's old friends Jim Wheeler and Chad Walldorf went straight to Columbia to spend the night with Mark and to try to convince him not to see Belen again. Jim lives in Florida, and he flew to meet Mark, and Chad drove two hours to do so. Each loyal friend acted out of wanting to see Mark make the right decisions. They were trying, as had I, to hold him accountable to the values he had espoused and to the man they knew him to be. They thought they'd made some headway: Each called to tell me that they believed Mark understood the pain and problems he had caused and that they believed him when he said he wouldn't see her again.

Cubby Culbertson—the old friend who left his own family and work for two days to babysit Mark in New York—also proved to be a dear friend to Mark during this time as he repeatedly counseled him to follow the moral code outlined in the Bible and to get his heart pointed in the right direction.

In the fateful June press conference, Mark would refer to Cubby as a "spiritual giant," and I know that Mark regretted letting these friends down. Mark had people in his camp willing to go to great lengths to keep him focused in the right direction, and he didn't listen to a single one. I'm still a little awestruck at Mark's inability to listen to all these good, honest, and devoted friends. Moreover, that Mark seemed to have lost track of their worth to him shows how disconnected he had become.

But when he went missing, thoughts that he was with his lover in Argentina or elsewhere dominated my mind. Those suspicions were the subject of phone calls with friends and members of his staff who had scraps of information that suggested he'd traveled to the Appalachian Trail. As a gut response, I worried otherwise or that if he was there, perhaps he was not alone. And while I had an impulse to cover for him, to perpetuate his lies to protect our children, in truth, I didn't know for certain what he was doing.

So, when the reporter asked me if I knew where my husband was, I answered truthfully that I had no idea. I have heard since from people who read that quote, which was published in newspapers all over the country, that they wondered what my tone of voice was when I delivered that remark. In my memory, my tone was even, unremarkable. I didn't want to set off any alarms. One of my favorite Bible verses is Colossians 4:6, "Let your speech always be with grace, seasoned with salt." I said that Mark had a book contract and that he had been distracted. I didn't tell the reporter the *nature* of that distraction, of course. I simply said Mark and I had agreed he needed time to get his head straight and that he hoped to write. I so wish he actually had been writing.

I have always told the boys that lies come from fear, from cowardice. During the campaigns when they would be upset because Mark's political opponents were trying anything they could to knock Mark down, Mark and I would tell them that the truth gives you a backbone, a reason to stand tall and the means to do so. This was a message I felt deeply. Perhaps the only thing dealt with less than honestly and openly in my childhood was fear. When Mom was sick, our parents tried to make it seem like her cancer was not a big deal. We all knew her sister had just died of the same cancer. Despite what our parents told us, we kids were all afraid. That denial, and the fear underneath it, distorted our family in ways I think none of us appreciated until much later.

I recently asked my sister Gier why she never stood up for me or took my side in a certain disagreement I had with my mother during our turbulent teen years. Ever the peacemaker, Gier explained that she wanted to take my side, but she was afraid Mom was going to die and she didn't want to do anything to upset her.

Her logic makes perfect sense to me now, as a woman who has matured to appreciate the many shades of gray that come with conflicting loyalties. I adore Gier in a way that is only deepened by understanding that childhood struggle she was engaged in to keep her mom alive. We were not raised in a way or in a time or place where we could sit together and express our fears about losing our mom. If Mom was going to deny her illness with a big smile on her face, a splash of lipstick, and a pretty silk scarf, who were we to drag her into the living room and force her to confront it? We were children, children who carried so much inside that we didn't know how to express. I know how uncomfortable it made all of us to hold what was essentially a lie inside our hearts and to cover over that fear with all sorts of justifications and fantasies that were as extreme as the reality.

My mother never let the challenges of life divert her from her main goals. As children, we had no idea how she suffered and what terrors kept her awake at night. Now that I am an adult who has dealt repeatedly with comparatively minor skin cancers of my own, I have such profound admiration for my mother's persevering spirit. As the only survivor of an experimental cancer treatment program twenty years ago, she is an inspiration to me today because of her positive spirit. She was a warrior in the face of certain death. Mom wants to do the things that make her feel alive and give her days meaning. She never wanted to appear as if she was just about to die. She has her sights set on living as long as she can and enjoying every minute. I can see now how she didn't want to worry us, and as an adult I can respect that approach.

When the crisis of Mark's infidelity hit our family, however, without question I knew I would handle it in a different way for our children. I would face it head on, openly and honestly.

When Mark left the beach to "get his head straight" we

had still not told the boys any specifics about the nature of the tension between Mark and me. Before he went missing I knew I needed to reveal more to them about our circumstances, despite the advice of many who admonished me not to talk to the boys, not to burden them. My goal was honesty, but not brutal honesty. The message was brutal enough without me adding my pain. Was it possible, given everything I was feeling, to be both truthful and kind? Of course I would be kind to the boys and respectful of their love for their father. I had to find a way to explain things to them that would allow them to continue to love their dad and not force them to hate him out of loyalty to me or a desire to protect me.

When I sat the boys down, I explained to them that I had discovered in January that their dad was having an affair.

"Did they have sex?" asked Bolton.

"Yes, that's what an affair is about," I said.

I told them they didn't know the woman and they had nothing to do with causing the affair nor could they have prevented it. It was not their fault. I also told them that I loved their dad and was hopeful that he would keep his word as he had looked me in the eyes and said "I will not see her" when he left.

"Mom, that would be a pretty big lie if he sees her," Blake said.

"Yes," I agreed, "it would be a very big lie."

I assured the boys that I would never leave them and that they shouldn't worry about a thing because I would work to provide whatever they might need in the future. I was a little teary when discussing this painful personal subject with them, but I also felt as if a weight had been lifted after I shared this secret with my precious sons. No child should have to learn such things, but I wanted them to be well prepared in case the story got out; I didn't want them to learn about Mark's affair from the television or the public. We prayed together for Mark, for the choices he would make.

A few days later when I had reason to believe Mark was with his lover, I decided to sit down with the boys again and to tell them her name was Belen Chapur and that she lived in Argentina. The children thought of the notes Mark had recently sent each of them.

"That's it. His notes were good-bye," Blake said.

I was crushed by the hurt they must have felt at learning of his betrayal, and also by their thinking he might abandon them. Then with such clairvoyance Bolton exclaimed, "Oh my gosh. This is going to be worse than Eliot Spitzer!"

Yes, I thought, *unfortunately it will be.*

It broke my heart to call Marshall in the Turks and Caicos, where he was working a brief summer job, and to tell him the same things over the phone, just before his seventeenth birthday. I wanted to be with him to give him a big hug, but I made sure someone there kept a close eye on him. I was thankful in a way that he would miss the coming circus at home. In another way, though, I missed him deeply and I know his brothers did too. We were facing this as a family and taking strength from each other as we confronted our situation and our feelings honestly. What a mix of feelings we had. We had the shame of the betrayal and the coming public humiliation, but we also had our faith, our love of Mark and our family. I could see the gray of the confusion of conflicting emotions as clearly as I could see some part of it as black and white.

If there is any overriding message from this summer that I wanted our boys to remember it was that you may choose your sin but you cannot choose the consequences. Actions and sin do have consequences. The full consequences of the choices Mark made are still being discovered. I hope, though, that my boys have learned that dishonesty rarely serves one well, and it is always better to "walk in the truth."

I have long understood the concept that things may not be right with my circumstances but "it is well with my soul." Horatio Spafford, the man who wrote that song, had an even greater challenge to face than I did. All four of his daughters drowned in the Atlantic Ocean on a ship coming home from France. One of the lines in that song is "When sorrows like sea billows roll; Whatever my lot, Thou has taught me to say, 'It is well, it is well, with my soul.'" My circumstances were less tragic, but obviously not great. But I too had a peace in my soul. With Mark gone, with him no longer beseeching me for permission to betray me further, I could listen without disturbances to the strong voice of my true spirit. I felt a peace that came from knowing that I had acted in the best manner I knew possible in this marriage, I had loved to the best of my ability. It is well with my soul. But I would be completely well if I could forgive Mark fully and move on freely. If he was with her again after this clear restriction, could I?

In the governor's mansion, Landon occasionally dressed the bust of Ibra Blackwood in a blue wig, swim goggles, and a hat for the amusement of our visitors. Governor Blackwood is beloved for pardoning all the inmates on his mansion staff one Christmas long ago. So the story goes, he hung small envelopes with certificates of pardon bearing the name of each of the inmates on the Christmas tree in the large drawing room. How I wish the simple act of forgiveness in everyday life was as easy as hanging an ornament on a tree.

Of course, it was easy for Governor Blackwood to pardon those inmates; whatever they had done had happened to someone else, a family or an individual who even years later might still be struggling to forgive the person who caused that crime. When someone errs against us or causes harm, it is in our basic nature to fight back or to right a wrong. Watch any two children at play together long enough and you are bound to see one snatch a toy or stick from the other. The response is immediate. The wronged child grabs the toy back or screams and bops the other child over the head. Rarely is forgiveness instinctive. Forgiveness has to be learned, and even practiced, until it is easier to be truly and fully given. I had practiced it plenty, and if Mark was with his mistress again, my ability to do so would be tested further.

In a way, being in the political life has helped. Holding a

grudge takes time and energy. When I thought back to that letter to the editor I wrote during Mark's first campaign for Congress, I marveled at the amount of energy I expended on something that, if it were to happen today, wouldn't inspire a response at all. I've grown to ignore the lies printed about my husband or about me and I no longer try to right such perceived wrongs. I found that if I kept matters unresolved or bottled up, I was more engaged with that person than if I had forgiven them. I didn't want to spend the little time I had engaged in grudges. The more I let go, the freer I felt.

Yet I was not at all free from the kind of hurt Mark had inflicted. He had lied right to my face and gone to see his lover. He had deceived me, disregarded my emotions, my needs, my desires, my basic integrity. And this lie hurt the boys immensely, in ways unfathomable to me on so many levels. I walked the beach and reminded myself daily and joyfully of who I was and how I had been blessed. Yes I was truly blessed. I could feel that part. While I felt a genuine impulse to forgive, this time I knew it would not be easy and would take time and effort.

Every time I attend mass, the congregation asks aloud to be forgiven as we recite the Lord's Prayer, "forgive us our trespasses as we forgive others who trespass against us." We seek forgiveness from above, while we simultaneously are grantors of forgiveness to those around us. Matthew 7:4–5 says, "How can you say to your brother, 'Let me take the speck out of your eye' when all the time there is a plank in your own eye?

You hypocrite, first take the plank out of your own eye, and then you will see clearly to remove the speck from your brother's eye." I would be a hypocrite in my own eyes and in the eyes of the Lord for asking for forgiveness for my sins while judging Mark as unforgivable. The ultimate judgment is not mine; it is in the Lord's hands.

So too, it is the Lord who is responsible for making things right in this world. Mark had become so self-absorbed that he was lost. He had become so focused on his will and his desire that he was blinded to his actions and their consequences in a connected world. I understood that if Mark acted sinfully, it was not up to me to make him right or to punish him for his behavior. Mark was in charge of his behavior and, though I understood many of the trials he has faced, I reminded myself that I couldn't presume to know the challenges he has within.

Still, I continued to struggle with the concept. If I didn't forgive him, it would be as if I were saying that what he had done was too painful, too humiliating for anyone to say to him in any form that what he had done was okay. As much as that is true, I reminded myself that it was not my responsibility to mete out judgment. Saying "I forgive you" is not the same as saying "what you have done is okay." If I continued to deny Mark my forgiveness, I would remain entangled in his emotions. I knew that I couldn't force myself into his heart by refusing to forgive him. He was supremely self-absorbed, involved in his own tragedy, the tragedy of his lost chance of happiness with his one true soul mate, or however he might characterize it. He was not concerned about my feelings. I had become an abstraction to him, an obstacle, and whether I forgave him or not was irrelevant to what he would do next. Forgiveness, then, was for me.

As I walked the beach on those mornings of profound struggle, I thought again and again of the substance behind a favorite quote from Desmond Tutu, "forgiveness is the grace by which you enable the other person to get up, and get up with dignity, to begin anew." Forgiveness really is a gift for each of us. It gave us the freedom to move forward happily, free from our unfortunate situation.

Mark and I had long ago planned to go to Coosaw for July 4 so our house at the beach had been rented for that week, soon after Mark had returned from Argentina. I didn't want to spend a week at Coosaw given what was going on between Mark and me. My Mom and Dad were in Chicago for the summer and offered to let me use their house in Florida. Wanting to make this week special for the boys, and needing the strength and support of friends for me, we headed to Florida with Frannie and her four kids and two extra kids in tow.

We loaded the cars with surfboards, golf clubs, and tennis rackets and off we went. Denise, an old roommate from my time in New York, flew to meet me from her home in DC as did another friend from New York, Melissa. My sister Gier and her oldest son Fitz traveled from Chicago. The eleven kids kept us busy cooking big meals between all of the activities. My sister and girlfriends kept me laughing whenever possible.

We were all together the day Mark called to tell me that he had more explaining to do. Another woman, it seemed, had come forward and suggested to a member of the press that she had also had relations with Mark, which meant he would likely have to address the accusation with an AP reporter who would be interviewing him later in the day. I was gut-punched all over again. Mark had sworn to me when I'd discovered his secret back in January that Belen was the only "other" woman. Now he explained that there had been nothing much at all with this new woman, nothing he had felt I needed to know about before. Ever businesslike, he wanted to know what I thought he should reveal in the interview. Here again he was asking for *my advice* instead of first considering how the news might make me feel. Here again he was only really admitting his indiscretions because the woman had come forward, forcing him to come clean. I would soon learn—secondhand from the AP interview—that Mark had had yet more dalliances over the years, but that in his opinion he had not "crossed the line" as he'd done with Belen. When I pressed him for details when I saw him a few days later, I understood fully that his and my definition of an appropriate line were not at all the same.

Discovering that he had flirted with the idea of other affairs and perhaps even acted on some of his impulses was in a way more devastating than the public humiliation of the press conference when he returned from Argentina. How long, I wondered, had I had my head in the sand? I couldn't help but think I had been deceived through the entire marriage, and for the first time in all that painful year I felt duped. Mark had handled me the way he'd tried to handle the press. He'd given me just enough information when he had to, but clearly he hadn't given me the whole story. Not back in January. And maybe not even now. How could I know? How would I ever really know? I despaired about being able to forgive this bigger, broader hurt. I was about as close to breaking as one can be. I was testy, grumpy, teary, and exhausted.

My sister and girlfriends put up with me and supported me every step of the way. They made sure I took care of myself and that I remained focused on the kids and on deciding what was to come next with the kids and the marriage. Denise even made sure I started thinking about my future. Emails and letters poured in from around the country. We heard about people forming Jenny Sanford support groups and some organization began hawking t-shirts and mugs with "Team Jenny" on them. Denise registered web sites in my name and applied for a trademark so I would be protected from people exploiting my name and my image. I don't know what I would have done in this time without these and other friends and their loyal and loving support. I needed them desperately and they came through brilliantly.

Mark joined us in Florida at the end of the week to help drive home, and I found him to be surprisingly devoid of true remorse, only regret for the outcomes. Needless to say, I was incredibly disappointed and our drive home was tolerable for me because I had Mark drive with Frannie, who remained mostly silent except for the boys in her car roughhousing and harassing each other in the back.

After we returned from Florida, feeling spent by Mark and simultaneously recharged by my friends, Mark and I went to an intense five-day marriage counseling session. I got a lot out of this marathon session—I learned a lot about Mark's psychology and a lot about my own as well. Day after day of talking about yourself and probing your motivations was helpful to me. I came home from the counseling hopeful for my future, whether with Mark or without, but also had a renewed willingness to work one last time to improve things, for the sake of our kids. Mark seemed distant still, but promised me that the trip to Europe we had planned for the next week near the end of that summer would be great for the two of us and the kids. I didn't really want to go to Europe, but I didn't want to disappoint the boys; they had been earning money to help pay for the trip and their dedicated efforts should, I felt, be rewarded. (Bolton had walked the beach selling lemonade and water from a cart and Blake sold lemonade and performed magic tricks [!] from a stand on the street while Landon painted part of the house.) At that point, I was committed to reconciliation, though not much in Mark's actions gave me reason to be hopeful for it. But Mark repeatedly promised he would *show me* how committed he was, and this family trip to Europe, I reasoned, would give him a chance to start doing so.

But there wasn't much time for him to demonstrate his professed new resolve. This was another jam-packed Sanford family vacation with a cruise from Venice to the Greek isles along with time in London, Paris, and the beaches of Normandy, all in less that two weeks. Mark was considerate and sweet to me the first two days, and then he was hot and cold for the rest of the vacation. All in all, I think he was wallowing in his self-pity and still pining for his girl, while also trying to go through the motions to keep the marriage together. By the end of the trip, I couldn't wait to get home.

Before heading to Europe, in anticipation of a possible more permanent move to the beach, I had hired a contractor to add some bookshelves and closets and to paint and restore the interior of the house after its years of summer rentals. My Mom came through like a superstar and made sure the workmen did as promised while we were away. She got the house put back in shape with new computer lines and freshened up bedrooms for the boys. This was no small task in a short time and I was so thankful to have her there in charge.

The boys each said Europe was the highlight of their summer, so I guess Mark and I were able to keep it together in their eyes. On the last day, however, we took the Chunnel from Paris to London and were recognized by a member of the press on the train. On arrival in London, there was a small pack of paparazzi waiting for us, and it broke my heart to have the boys see Mark hounded like a criminal.

One thing was clear to me when we got back. Mark hadn't yet convinced me that he would be the least bit different in our marriage going forward. As soon as we got back to Columbia, therefore, I told the boys that we were moving back to the beach for the foreseeable future and that they would be changing schools. My not-so-secret hope was that Mark would be lonely in the big mansion by himself and that he'd glimpse the future that would be his if he continued to be so remote and unrepentant. Mark wasn't keen on the idea of us moving—he would miss us, he said, and he thought the move punished him too much—but he backed me up in order to present a united front to the boys. The boys were not wild about the move either, but with their parents in agreement, we started to prep for it.

I didn't look forward to having to move, but as it turned out, I had pleasant surprises in store for me. All I had to do was tell a few girlfriends of my planned move and they went into action. Some put fresh flowers in the pots at the beach so the house would feel lived in. Others showed up with garbage bags to help move things from the mansion, and another crew met us at the beach as we arrived. Mom smiled at me in the kitchen as the camera trucks waited for a tidbit of news at the end of the driveway. Mark had taken the boys to Coosaw for two days so that they wouldn't have to be a part of the chaos of the move, and so they too were pleasantly surprised to find peace, calm, and, to top it all off, private bedrooms at long last (and for the first time in their lives!) for Marshall and Landon.

If nothing else, this crisis has taught me never to take my friends for granted. Not that I ever have taken them for granted, but it reminded me that there are times in life when we absolutely need friends. We need to love them and we need to listen to them. Likewise there are times when we need our family. We can easily get into a position where we think we can do so much on our own, and often we can, but we are not meant to live alone. I can only imagine where I would be this very moment and what our family and future would be like if Mark had listened to and respected the advice of his dear friends instead of following his "heart."

FOURTEEN

Nothing rejuvenates my spirit more than a walk along the shore. Watching the willets scamper at the edge of the water as the tide ebbs calms me and makes me feel closer to God. In the quiet, unstructured time that comes when I can be still and soak up the wonders of His creation, it is difficult to feel anger or to wallow in my suffering. My daily walks there help me put my life in perspective, all of its insignificance, and all of His goodness.

Now that the boys and I have settled at the beach, we have relaxed into a comfortable rhythm. I am up early reading and then getting their breakfast. Then they race through their meals, and Marshall herds them into his truck. A few minutes later, they are peeling out of the driveway, gravel spraying, as they dash off to school. Then lovely peace, and hours ahead where I can think, or write, grocery shop or see a friend. But first, I can hear the beach calling to me as I open the gate to the path there. With each step I take away from the house, I release. Release from the bills to be paid, laundry to be folded, scraped knees to be kissed, and dreams, dreams yet to dream, let alone fulfill. And what of the dreams for our marriage that the house once contained? Who was I to Mark and who was he to me?

Daily chores mix with questions, images, and memories that sometimes distract me from what really matters and how I truly feel. Near the end of the path, my steps quicken with eagerness for the sea and the sense of order it can give to a disordered mind. And then I am there, with the Atlantic stretched wide before me. The sense of timelessness and the beauty I feel in this space helps me cultivate my faith.

There are days when I feel supported by its peace, charmed by the brightness as the foamy edges of waves timidly advance across the sand. Other days the sea is violent, tumultuous, aggressive with gritty wind and cold spray. Sometimes I look out across its peaceful and unruffled surface and wonder what turmoil remains below. The sea allows a world of contradictions. Tossed around by contradictions, I am steadied by my faith.

Faith is waking up every day with an attitude of gratitude, knowing that, as I once wrote in my journal, "This is the day the Lord has made, let us rejoice and be glad in it!" These were the thoughts that steadied me in this tumultuous year when my world fell to pieces. My pain was so intense and the future horribly uncertain, I took my faith from watching the sun set and knowing it surely would rise again, or watching the tides rush out, knowing the waters would flow back in. At that moment, faith needed to be just that simple for me to receive comfort from it, as everything I believed had suddenly shown itself to be untrue.

There were times when I walked with swift determination, in a heart-pounding frenzy, to shake these feelings out of me. Other walks, I went slowly, pausing to absorb the vastness. On days filled with turmoil and doubt, I wanted to know, to feel, that these problems were insignificant spread out across this calm expanse. I didn't always find peace there quickly, but my faith kept me searching until I did.

In July, just a few weeks after Mark's visit to Argentina, I was returning from a long walk on the beach when I saw a young woman helped to shore and saw the Sullivan's Island rescue squad speed out in search of another. The sea had stripped the woman of her clothes, and another woman had wrapped her in a t-shirt and towel. I hurried over to help comfort her. She said the friend she had been swimming with was not from the area, and had thought she knew how to handle the strong currents but proved not to be as strong a swimmer. The other woman and I prayed for her and for her lost friend. When it became clear that she was in good hands, I hurried home to make sure my boys were safe.

I called Marshall, who was with his brothers, and all were accounted for and safe at a nearby park. I began to cook dinner, watching the rescue helicopters as they circled in vain, searching for a young life. I thought, Lord I am listening. . . . what are you telling me? I began to sing happily while I made spaghetti. I have a beautiful home, a good life, and wonderful, happy, bright children. I have great friends and a loving family. I am fine and I am blessed beyond belief. In my journal the next day I wrote of joy: "Find joy every day. My problems are insignificant." I prayed, Psalm 139: "Search me, O God and know my heart; test me and know my anxious thoughts. See if there is any offensive way in me and lead me in the way everlasting." My heart has been pained but it is clean and I have peace. I have so much gratitude, there is no space, even in this vastness, for one drop of bitterness or regret.

I have many good girlfriends on the island, as well as my sister and friends nearby. On weekends, we often sit together while the kids tumble around. There are often communal dinners where someone brings a salad and someone else gets something on the grill. There seems now to be enough time for everything and yet each of these moments is too precious to waste. It is not perfect, but we have found balance.

I have been unwavering in my quest for understanding—for growth, knowledge, wisdom, and discernment. This has been true throughout my life and my marriage and certainly through these trying personal times. I have been patient and worked hard not to judge rashly or quickly but rather to understand, to learn. And I have learned. I learned that I need others to help and support me in trying times. I am vulnerable. I have learned just how loved I am. My family and friends have been incredible. My faith has remained strong and my God ever loving. I have also learned just how great and resilient our boys are and how undeserving of this crisis they truly are.

I have loved and will love again. I have lived these married years as loyally, as honestly, as lovingly and as committed as I could. I have worked hard and enjoyed our successes. I have given of myself, have been blessed with incredible friendships, and have worked on building character—mine and our children's. With the strength of my faith and the blessings in my midst I am ready for the next chapter of my life where I hope to fully live each day, love each moment, and find joy along the way. I have known that character, self-respect, and integrity are so difficult to develop and earn and so easy to lose. I have tried my best to act responsibly, patiently, and fairly and will freely welcome the next chapter with no regrets from the past and no fears for the future. I will persevere with my feet firmly planted—preferably with some sand between my toes—focused on my priorities and looking onward and ever upward.

ACKNOWLEDGMENTS

One of the incredible blessings of life in the public eye has been, for me, the outpouring of support from people of all walks of life across South Carolina and even from some across the nation. These are people who have helped us and our family in different ways throughout the various campaigns we have endured or through Mark's time in office or trials along the way. Some licked envelopes or volunteered their time, others raised or donated money, some sent notes of support or said encouraging words on the street, and countless told us they were praying for us. In all the years of public service, I never felt as if we walked alone. For that I will remain forever grateful. This book would not be possible without your collective support.

Of course, this book would not be on shelves without the

able help of my editor, Marnie Cochran; my publisher, Libby McGuire; my collaborator, Danelle Morton; and my agent, Joy Tutela. A fine team of strong women. We worked together beautifully, happily, and in record time—a real accomplishment. My thanks to you all.

The people who have helped me on this incredible journey of life are too numerous to mention by name but I would not be where I am today without your constant love and support. My family, especially my parents, have been unfailing cheerleaders and a great safety net. My girlfriends, from all the various stages and places in my life, have been so loyal and always there to laugh together, give a hug, share a smile, or lend a shoulder to cry on. I appreciate you all more than you know.

My boys have been a constant source of love and joy, and they are my greatest legacy. I am grateful for each one of them.

And finally I am thankful for the many blessings I have received from my God, and most of all for His unfailing love.

ABOUT THE AUTHOR

JENNY SULLIVAN SANFORD was born and raised in Winnetka, Illinois. A graduate of Georgetown University, she now lives on Sullivan's Island, South Carolina, with her four sons.

ABOUT THE TYPE

This book was set in Electra, a typeface designed for Linotype by W. A. Dwiggins, the renowned type designer (1880–1956). Electra is a fluid typeface, avoiding the contrasts of thick and thin strokes that are prevalent in most modern typefaces.